Facilitating Youth-Led Book Clubs as Transformative and Inclusive Spaces

T0384322

Facilitating Youth-Led Book Clubs as Transformative and Inclusive Spaces

Jody Polleck

TEACHERS COLLEGE PRESS

TEACHERS COLLEGE | COLUMBIA UNIVERSITY

NEW YORK AND LONDON

Published by Teachers College Press,® 1234 Amsterdam Avenue, New York, NY 10027

Front cover painting by Devin Osorio.

Library of Congress Cataloging-in-Publication Data

Names: Polleck, Jody, author.
Title: Facilitating youth-led book clubs as transformative and inclusive spaces / Jody Polleck.
Description: New York, NY : Teachers College Press, 2022. | Includes bibliographical references and index. | Summary: "Learn how to use book clubs with adolescents to enhance and nurture their literacies, along with their social and emotional development"—Provided by publisher.
Identifiers: LCCN 2022010902 (print) | LCCN 2022010903 (ebook) | ISBN 9780807767504 (paperback) | ISBN 9780807767511 (hardback) | ISBN 9780807781302 (ebook)
Subjects: LCSH: Reading (Secondary)—United States. | Group reading—United States. | Book clubs (Discussion groups)—United States. | Transformative learning—United States.
Classification: LCC LB1632 .P65 2022 (print) | LCC LB1632 (ebook) | DDC 418/.40712—dc23/eng/20220425

LC record available at https://lccn.loc.gov/2022010902
LC ebook record available at https://lccn.loc.gov/2022010903

ISBN 978-0-8077-6750-4 (paper)
ISBN 978-0-8077-6751-1 (hardcover)
ISBN 978-0-8077-8130-2 (ebook)

Printed on acid-free paper
Manufactured in the United States of America

This book is dedicated to all the youth I have had the honor of learning from. I am forever grateful for our conversations and connections.

Also to Gordon Pradl: Without your mentorship and guidance, this book would never have been possible. May your legacy of pedagogical prowess and generosity continue to inspire us all.

Proceeds of this book will go to the Native American Rights Fund and the NAACP Legal Defense and Educational Fund.

Contents

Acknowledgments

I wrote this book for two primary reasons: to honor youth voices and to share strategies for how we can use book clubs to enact change within our school communities. I also wrote this book because I hope—and I hope audaciously (Duncan-Andrade, 2009). I hope for more equitable school systems, I hope this book will help at least one community in their methods of supports, I hope I continue to grow and develop, and I hope for my students—that they will continue to read, connect, and use the experiences of book clubs to create a better world.

This book is, first and foremost, for every student I have had the privilege of working with. I thank you for your investment, compassion, intellect, and vision. Special thanks to Devin Osorio, a champion many moons ago in our lunchtime book clubs. Your design for this book cover captures the magic and joy we experienced together.

I next want to acknowledge the mental health specialists whom I have worked with over the years. Thank you, Yolanda Pounds and Danilo Martinez. You rest in my heart and mind as I write about and engage with youth. May your brilliance and compassion continue to heal others. I also want to acknowledge Joan Kaywell for introducing me to bibliotherapy, and to my writing partner, Tadashi Dozono, for reading every word of this manuscript and helping me to grow as a writer and critical scholar. Thank you also to Eli Mashkow for your feedback and for creating a website that will keep this book fresh and innovative.

To my colleagues and friends who have touched this text and supported me since its inception: David Connor, Darrell Hucks, Nicora Placa, Jen Samson, and Melissa Schieble. I also want to thank those of you who read the early drafts, offering insights on the content and writing. Your perspectives and expertise make this book a collective triumph. Much appreciation to Matthew Blake, Tanya Friedman, Samantha Jacob, Alexa Lee, Mallory Locke, Lina Rahmani, and Anderson Smith. I must also pay special tribute to the scholars who have guided my work, most especially Shawn Ginwright, Bettina Love, Django Paris, and Dena Simmons. I also want to express my deep gratitude to the Provost Office of Hunter College and the CUNY Research Foundation for their financial support. Many thanks to Teachers College Press and, most notably, my editor Emily Spangler, who has been so generous and supportive since that day I nervously walked into her office on Amsterdam Avenue.

Finally, to my husband Michael: There is not a large enough word count in the world. Thank you for listening to me read aloud every week, for helping me push through my ideas, for challenging my insecurities, for your eagerness to celebrate as I finished each of these chapters, and for lifting me up. You are my Gibraltar.

CHAPTER 1

Transformation and Inclusivity

The Foundation for Student-Centered Book Clubs

I am sitting in a conference room in the main office of my New York City high school, and it is my favorite time of the week: book club. Gathered around a table are five adolescent women who eagerly eat their pizza off flimsy paper plates. They are Fay, Sofia, Joy, Betsy, and Tia*—and today, they have chosen to read the first chapter of *Tiger Eyes* (Blume, 2010). It's an outdated book to be sure, but in our last session together, I explained that when I was their age, this was the text that helped me feel less isolated.

Sharing my background, I told them about how my father died when I was young and how my mother and I spent much of our time together, while she worked three jobs and I huddled in corners of her various places of work, reading books to escape or to understand myself. As a child, while living in tiny apartments and trailer parks throughout the South, I read Nancy Drew while my mom waited tables; I read Agatha Christie while she worked as an x-ray technician at a public hospital; and I read Judy Blume on the weekends as she groomed dogs in the back of a beat-up van.

I explained that I read to escape—to avoid thinking about my loss or how we were going to pay rent that month. I explained I also read for connection—so I could see myself in the texts I read, to understand my life and experiences. Bishop (1990) refers to these interactions as mirrors, windows, and sliding glass doors, where students experience real or imagined—new or connected—worlds, where they enter the story and see their identities and communities throughout the pages.

I took a risk with these young women, sharing my vulnerabilities and telling them about my life as a child coping with death and being raised in a single-parent, low-income household. I also shared how reading helped me process trauma and that those books served as refuge to help me cope with my own struggles.

I intended to use *Tiger Eyes* as a model for how I connected with books. Sharing my experiences was a way to give these young women windows into

---

* All student names are pseudonyms.

1

my life so that perhaps in the future, they might be comfortable sharing their stories too.

Curious, Fay asked, "Do you think we could read this one together? I mean, would you want to read it again?"

Given the setting of the book (New Mexico) and the time period (1980s), I did not think this was a text I would ever read with my students. I also didn't think these five young women, all Black and Latinx, all from New York City, would be interested; I thought the book too dated, too white, too suburban—all aspects of my identity that differed from theirs. I also knew that though we shared some similarities, I could never fully understand their experiences as young women of color. I also knew that my privilege allowed me to navigate my life and these traumas in much easier ways due to my whiteness.

But the girls all agreed with Fay. They wanted to try the first chapter. So, we read the opening pages, where we learn that the main character, Davey, is about to attend her father's funeral.

After I finish the last sentence of the chapter, the young women and I open our journals and respond to our initial feelings about the text. When I ask who wants to share, the room becomes quiet and I get nervous, yet again, thinking that reading this book was a mistake. But Betsy bravely breaks the silence, declaring, "I'll read my journal entry."

She pauses, takes a deep breath, and begins: "It's really hard to see your parent die and watch the body being lowered into the ground."

Betsy's hands shake a bit, and she stops reading, looking nervously at her fingers, which are now in her lap. She continues, though, looking up briefly: "When my mother died, I was young. I couldn't stand seeing my mother being dead. I thought this was not reality, and I was waking up from a bad dream. But this dream has been going on for seven years. And I still haven't woken up from it. I felt like I couldn't relate to anybody because nobody understood what I was talking about, and my family acted—well, they didn't act like it was sad. They acted like they knew it was coming, but I didn't and to see my mother just lying there all stiff. I didn't know what to do."

When Betsy finishes, I thank her for her courage and share that I too experienced many of those same feelings when my father passed. I tell her that she is not alone and that we are grateful for her sharing. I then ask the group if anyone else wanted to read from their journals. Again, a long silence ensues. Fay, the smallest in the group, with black-framed glasses, pushes them up the bridge of her nose and says, "I'll share but I'm not gonna read from my journal. I said, this book reminded me of when my mother died. I was young too, but unlike the character, I was crying a lot, and I didn't understand what death was. I just—you know when you have a feeling that they're not going to be there anymore? It made me so sad. At that time, I didn't know anything at all. I didn't know I had sisters and brothers; I didn't even know who my father was. I didn't know anybody and everything happened so fast."

I am in shock at this moment. I didn't know about either of the young women's experiences with death as we had just met last month. It was my first year at the school as a literacy coach, and for them, as entering ninth-graders, their first year as well. I worried that in this moment I might be stirring up trauma by sharing pieces of myself and with reading this book aloud.

But then I remember in global history, they are reading about colonization and slavery. In English, they are reading *Romeo and Juliet*. As a teacher, I question, am I prepared to have these conversations with youth? I feel my face grow hot as a heavy stone of guilt and uncertainty coagulates in my core.

But Betsy and Fay do not miss a beat. They begin to speak to each other about how gutting the losses were for them but also how joyful it was to be reunited with their fathers, who are now solid and supportive figures in their lives. Betsy says to Fay, "I never met someone who went through this too."

Meanwhile, Sofia, Tia, and Joy listen as Betsy and Fay converse, interjecting here and there with nods and encouraging smiles. Eventually, they too share their experiences with death and how difficult loss has been in their lives. I am there, mostly listening but also secretly wishing that when I was in high school, I could have found a group of people who understood fatality and were courageous enough to speak to their vulnerabilities.

I also knew at that point that I had a lot to learn. That if I believed in the power of book clubs as a space for joy, inclusivity, and transformation, then I had to do the work. This meant a deep commitment to culturally sustaining curriculum. It meant learning about trauma-informed and healing-centered approaches (Ginwright, 2018; Simmons, 2019). It meant challenging my privileges and reflecting daily about my interactions with youth. It meant reaching out to the experts in my community, the social workers, families, and paraprofessionals who could help me navigate and sustain these spaces.

Therein lies the beginning of my work with book clubs. I thank you, the readers, who have the interest and the commitment, who have taken the time to read about what I've learned from these young people about ways that we can use texts and the communal spaces of book clubs to provide inclusive and transformative forums where we can address students' academic and social-emotional development. Welcome. I am grateful for you being here with me.

WHAT HAS BEEN MY JOURNEY TO BOOK CLUBS?

I come to this book with humility and gratitude. As a white, cisgender, able-bodied woman born in the United States, I continually work to understand my privileges and combat assumptions and biases. For more than 25 years, I have worked within urban settings with culturally, linguistically, and neurologically diverse students. I am deeply committed to creating equitable communities, but I also know that I am not infallible, and I have and will make mistakes along the way. I will share those on our journey together to be transparent and reflective about the decisions that we make as people who serve youth.

My career began in 1994 when I was an outreach counselor for displaced young adults in Washington, D.C. Through years of conversations with these adolescent sex workers, I learned from them that neither their homes nor their schools were safe spaces. Nor did they experience educational communities where they could speak to others about the challenges in their lives. Especially for the LGBTQ youth I met, many felt safer once they stopped attending school.

After 3 years in this position, I returned to Florida to be closer to my mother, who needed support. There, I brought what I learned from the youth in D.C. to my master's program in English education. In 1998, I began my life's work as a teacher, seeking to create classrooms for safety and community. Borrowing from Espinoza's research (2009) with migrant youth, I wanted to create spaces that could serve as sanctuaries. Espinoza discusses the importance of creating social spaces, particularly for marginalized students, where youth have opportunities for collaboration and experience humanization.

For the last 20 years, I have facilitated and researched book clubs worldwide with culturally and linguistically diverse students with various abilities. This book will capture that journey, centering their voices as they engaged with texts and each other. Focusing on adolescent, secondary students, I will share research that supports holistic approaches while also providing practical and flexible strategies so that book clubs can be inclusive of our students' diverse needs.

At the same time, I will lean into areas of discomfort and vulnerability. Considering my position of privilege, I want to embrace areas of challenge so that my approaches for book clubs are explicit and transparent. I acknowledge and understand my identity's inherently problematic nature in working with minoritized and marginalized youth. Daily, I am reflective of and work against white savior narratives. However, fear of these perceptions and realities should not extinguish my stories, nor my commitment to dismantling systems of oppression. Thus, I hear the calling from Matias and Mackey (2016), who ask white teachers to shoulder the burdens of discrimination and oppression, by not viewing themselves as saviors but instead transforming their privileged identities to "racial justice advocates" (p. 48). While I cannot extricate my whiteness, my cisgender identification, my abled body, nor my other identities of privilege, I can offer experiences of my growth. I share these not to center myself, but to be transparent about the critical work of self-reflection. Nieto (2016) explains that we cannot negate our own "identity and power when interacting with students," but we can try to understand our identity as "intertwined" with the students we teach (p. 126).

A large part of this work for me has involved my commitment to diverse literature, the core of book clubs. Returning to Bishop (1990), she warns us that "when children cannot find themselves in the books that they read, or when the images they see are distorted, negative, or laughable, they learn a powerful lesson about how they are devalued in the society of which they are part" (p. 9). So along with Judy Blume, the young women introduced in the opening vignette also engaged with authors such as Jacqueline Woodson, Rita Williams-Garcia, Esmeralda Santiago, and Kalisha Buckhanon—all literary pillars who provide windows, sliding glass doors, and mirrors for youth.

As people who work with diverse youth and their intersectional identities, there will be times when our stories and experiences overlap; yet often they will not. We must be reflective when this occurs, considering how our positionalities impact youth and their families. We must commit, personally and professionally, to work through these areas of dissonance, while using privileges to advocate for and with our students. In not reflecting on our positionalities, we may create more harm, thus further marginalizing vulnerable populations. Love (2019) explains that to provide freedom for all students, we must welcome struggle: "There are no saviors. There is only a village, a community, and a goal: protecting children's potential" (pp. 82–83). So, I ask you, as the reader, to be my collaborator on this journey, to imagine book clubs where dominant and mainstream narratives are decentered and inclusivity is focal, where we create in collaboration with students and their families spaces for resistance and love that sustain and nurture the wealth of our students' identities.

WHAT ARE BOOK CLUBS?

Book clubs are groups of readers who read texts and come together to discuss them regularly. Ultimately these forums should be student-led, with facilitators there for guidance and support. Book clubs have also been called literature circles, reading clubs, literature study groups, student-led book conversations, or literature discussion groups (Cherry-Paul & Johansen, 2019; Pittman & Honchell, 2014). They look very different depending on the students, the context, the facilitator, and the purpose. Thus, this book will provide multiple examples of ways facilitators can work with diverse populations within diverse contexts.

The two critical components of all book clubs are the reading and the conversations that ensue. The process of reading provides youth with opportunities to see themselves in the text or to expose them to different identities, communities, and experiences. The process of discussion allows students to share and renegotiate those interpretations to have richer understandings of the texts, themselves, and their communities. Both the reading and discussion processes provide youth with multiple perspectives, either through the characters or their peers, to achieve a more nuanced and richer understanding of issues that matter to them.

Figure 1.1 offers a visual representation of the processes I will describe in this book. The book club relies first on the texts themselves, which students read independently or collaboratively. Rosenblatt (1994) calls this a transaction, where readers engage with the text and participate in meaning construction. During the reading process, students' literacies develop along with their

Figure 1.1. Transformative Process of Inclusive Book Clubs

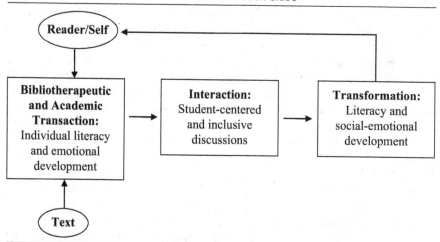

emotions, especially as they learn from the characters and their motivations and actions. When students then interact with one another, within student-centered and inclusive book clubs, the experience can become transformative, as youth share their responses and connections to the texts and to each other. Through strong and intentional facilitation, we can navigate these spaces where students begin to integrate what they've learned from the books and their peers into their own lives and communities. The transformative experiences of book clubs can potentially change the reader—so that they think about and interact with books and their communities perhaps differently than they did before. Later in this book, I will return to these processes in more detail. For now, it is important to notice the cyclical and recursive nature of book clubs.

Further, book clubs vary depending on the context of our communities—and, thus, they can be facilitated in many different ways and by many different people. Facilitators can include teachers, counselors, social workers, caregivers, administrators, parent coordinators, paraprofessionals, speech pathologists, and other school personnel. Ultimately, we want our students to become the facilitators so that the spaces are student-centered and student-led, which empowers them to engage with texts and one another in ways that best meet their needs.

And so, this book is for all of you.

For those with a wide range of experiences. From the person who has never been in a book club to the person who drinks wine once a month with a group of friends who have all read the same book. From the person who has never taught a class to the person who has done literature circles for years in their own classrooms.

In this book, I will offer several examples of book clubs facilitated by people of many different educational positionalities, both in and outside of the brick and mortar of schools. We will look at book clubs in classrooms, conference rooms, libraries, bookstores, and digital spaces. And I will do my best to meet you where you are and build on what you already do.

I just ask that we always keep in mind our students first, specifically their diversities, positionalities, interests, and needs. Remember that their safety and sense of community are always the priority, as we want to ensure that the spaces we co-create and co-facilitate truly center students' voices and concerns.

WHAT DOES IT MEAN TO BE TRANSFORMATIVE AND INCLUSIVE?

The title of this text describes book clubs as inclusive and transformative. But what do I mean by these terms? Let's start with inclusivity. According to UNESCO (2017), educational opportunities must be afforded to *all* students, and exclusionary access should be prohibited based on gender, ethnicity, race, language, religion, economic conditions, sexuality, and abilities. Inclusive approaches ensure that educational systems remove barriers, eliminate discrimination, and allow equitable participation and achievement for all learners. Inclusive, however, does not mean folding students into mainstream, dominant narratives. It means elevating the voices of *all* young people so they feel seen, heard, and valued.

This book will help us develop and refine inclusive practices within our communities through the processes of book clubs. While these approaches can be used for all students, I will center the lived experiences of those historically and currently marginalized. Marginalized youth have experienced systemic discrimination, based on their race, ethnicity, class, gender, language, sexuality, and ability. This includes youth of color, native and Indigenous youth, immigrant and refugee youth, youth with dis/abilities, and youth who identify as LGBTQ.

I also define book clubs as transformative. An activist and educator for impoverished peoples in Brazil, Freire (1993) believed in and used practices that were transformative and liberating. In direct contrast to the "banking" concept of education, where students are viewed and treated as vessels who learn from their teachers, Freire offers us the concept of *problem-posing education*, which allows for increased freedom of interpretation by situating the facilitator (in this case, book clubs) and students as equals in dialogue to make meaning. Transformative spaces break down hierarchies between adult and adolescent, where transparency, vulnerability, and authenticity are critical practices for all. Questions and topics thus come from students—and dialogue for cognition, liberation, and collaboration are central to the work. Further, to be transformative, all participants engage in both reflection *and* action.

This book will describe how to create forums that are inclusive and transformative, spaces where students can share their textual interpretations and how these connect to their identities and communities. Their reflective conversations about books serve as catalysts where they begin to see transformation and change in characters—and ultimately transfer these learnings and insights to their own lived experiences.

This book will also elucidate how these spaces are about hope, where students can bring to book clubs their successes and challenges to not only speak to these issues, but to feel empowered to change how they engage with the world.

Duncan-Andrade (2009) describes the premise of "critical hope," which demands we actively commit to working against inequities. Book clubs allow students and facilitators alike to examine their lives and communities—to reveal the struggles and the pain—that may ultimately "pave the path to justice" (p. 188). Thus, book clubs are centrally about nurturing hope and solidarity while working toward building our students' capacity for collaborative healing, academic development, and agency.

WHY DO WE NEED BOOK CLUBS?

U.S. researchers (Twenge, Martin, & Spitzberg, 2019) surveyed over one million middle and high school students from 1976 to 2016, finding that students read significantly less than they did 40 years ago. Further, students' dispositions and motivations for reading, whether academic or recreational, decrease significantly when they reach middle school (McKenna, Conradi, Lawrence, Jang, & Meyer, 2012). Only 16% of 12th-graders in 2016 engaged in daily reading of books or magazines, and less than a third of 13-year-olds are reading daily (Organization for Economic Co-operation and Development [OECD], 2011). This translates to students experiencing much less time with print, which increases challenges when youth enter college and career. Twenge, Spitzberg, and Campbell (2019) also found that adolescents are spending much less time interacting with their peers in person, which may be correlated with their increased use of digital and social media. The researchers also revealed that adolescents' sense of loneliness has increased dramatically, especially for females, Black and Latinx youth, and students from low socioeconomic households.

Worldwide, students are facing other challenges, from poverty and violence to inequitable schools and discrimination. I propose in this book that not only can book clubs be spaces where students and facilitators spend more time with text and with their peers, but also these forums can provide space for youth to interrogate their problems collectively. To be clear, book clubs should not be positioned as ways to close "achievement gaps"—as this continual focus on gaps holds us prisoners to deficit paradigms. Ladson-Billings (2007) cautions us of achievement gap language in that this discourse ignores the systemic access gaps to healthcare, wealth, housing, and schools, which impact our most vulnerable students.

Instead, Ladson-Billings (2007) asks us to consider educational debts, which means we are accountable to our students and their families. Viewing schools as places of educational debt forces us to recognize and address the inequities in our schools, particularly for students of color, students with dis/abilities, and students who identify as LGBTQ. Although book clubs will not cure our worldwide racist, sexist, trans/homophobic, ableist, and xenophobic institutional structures, they can be used as powerful spaces to interrogate, resist, and plan for actions that are needed to help our students survive and thrive in a world that may work against them.

WHAT ARE THE BENEFITS OF BOOK CLUBS?

In general, when we engage students in reading, research tells us that their academic achievement overall increases (Guthrie, Wigfield, & You, 2012; OECD, 2011), as does their social and emotional growth (Ivey & Johnston, 2013). In the last 2 decades, much research has also arisen demonstrating how book clubs can help increase adolescent academic and social-emotional development. For example, in my studies, I found that book clubs helped build students' social-emotional capacities while enhancing their reading dispositions, particularly for youth of color, youth from low socioeconomic neighborhoods, and youth with dis/abilities (Tijms, Stoop, & Polleck, 2018). Similarly, Choi and Sachs (2016) worked with groups of multilingual students and found that book clubs not only helped their development of English but also provided them with spaces for cultural exchanges, where they could learn about ethnic and religious differences.

In terms of isolated academic benefits, when looking at students' literacy skills and dispositions, book clubs can improve

- reading skills as they connect to Common Core Standards (Polleck, 2016);
- reading comprehension, with such skills as visualizing, connecting, questioning, inferring, and analyzing (Ketch, 2005);
- reading achievement scores (Daniels, 2002);
- appreciation for reading (Allington & Cunningham, 2007); and
- reflective reading behaviors (Sanacore, 2013).

Other academic skills, beyond literacy, are also enhanced within book clubs. Research has demonstrated that book clubs can help increase students'

- engagement with content (Gibbons, Dail, & Stallworth, 2006);
- critical and high-level thinking and reasoning skills (Pittman & Honchell, 2014); and
- motivation (Schreuder & Savitz, 2020; Williams, 2009).

For students who may be reading below grade level or for youth who are not engaged in reading books yet, book clubs can increase their enjoyment of reading while also enhancing their comprehension. Taber, Woloshyn, and Lane (2012), for example, worked with adolescent females who were reading below grade level and found that book clubs enhanced their confidence and motivation to read while also allowing them to engage in critical conversations around gender inequities. Blum, Lipsett, and Yocum (2002) found that book clubs helped increase reading comprehension for neurodiverse students, while other researchers demonstrated book clubs can be impactful with the language and literacy development of emergent bi- and multilingual students (Early & Marshall, 2008; Elhess & Egbert, 2015).

Book clubs can also increase students' engagement with their peers and provide them with social outlets. These forums offer youth opportunities for positive social interactions and discussions around issues that matter to them. These collaborative spaces also allow for co-construction of meaning, which deepens students' understanding and connection to the texts they read together.

Book clubs also help students develop deeper interpersonal relationships with others. In my research, I found that book clubs helped youth collaboratively problem-solve a myriad of personal issues, specifically as they discussed and negotiated relationships with their peers and families (Polleck, 2011a, 2011b).

Research has also emerged around how book clubs increase students' awareness of multiculturalism and how they can be used to prepare youth to live in diverse societies (Daniels, 2002). Book clubs, for example, are spaces for youth to grapple with identity, language, race, sexuality, social class, and gender in that they encourage students to take on more critical perspectives (Sanacore, 2013). Specifically, Broughton's (2002) research found that book clubs enhanced Latinxs' understanding of themselves, while Vyas (2004) found that they helped Asian students experiencing a sense of identity duality.

Further, by using texts that center the experiences of diverse peoples and characters, book clubs have enabled youth of color to explore their historical legacies and increase their confidence and self-esteem (Boston & Baxley, 2007; Fisher, 2006). These forums also provide space where youth can discuss topics such as discrimination (Brooks, Browne, & Hampton, 2008) to enhance their sense of agency (Polleck & Epstein, 2015).

The research is clear and robust: Book clubs can provide inclusive and transformative experiences for young people, especially when considering those who are most marginalized within our communities and schools.

WHO ARE BOOK CLUBS FOR?

This book will focus on the experiences of adolescent and secondary students. While certainly we can apply the strategies and approaches in this book to primary and elementary school-aged children, the students highlighted here will range in ages from 12 to 21. Considering the focus population, it is important to explore the concept of adolescence so that we are reflective of our assumptions and biases of youth and youth culture.

What comes to mind when you hear the word *adolescent* or *teen*? What kinds of images and behaviors do you see? Where do these constructions come from—and how do they impact the ways you engage with youth?

As facilitators of youth book clubs, we need to put aside a single definition for "adolescence." Youth vary based on experience, identity, and community—and it is important that we resist the urge to essentialize them. When we do, we place them into boxes and cannot see past deficit stereotypes that have been perpetuated within our communities and the media.

Critical scholarship around adolescence resists single biological or psychological views of youth, as we do not want to silence the social, cultural, neurological, linguistic, and historical differences among our students (Lesko, 2012; Sarigianides, 2012). In viewing adolescents with a monolithic lens, we fail to tap into their complexities and diversities. Further, these narrow adolescent developmental lenses have been problematic, as often adolescent constructs are informed by Western ideologies—and therefore normative views of adolescence ignore our students' diversities and intersectionalities (Sulzer & Thein, 2016). Monolithic lenses of adolescents also tend to be heteronormative and disregard our students' diverse languages, literacies, cultures, and abilities.

We must then consider the intersectionalities of our students' identities. Developed by Crenshaw in the 1970s, awareness of intersectionality allows us to see the inequities that youth experience based not just on their gender and race but on how those intersect with each other and with other "identity-based systems of oppression" such as class, disability, sexuality, and language (Bell, 2016, p. 38). Lorde (2007) reminds us, "There is no such thing as a single issue struggle because we do not live single issue lives" (p. 138).

As you read this book, consider the students in these pages and their identities and communities. Then think about your identity and your students' diversities. How do our lives intersect and overlap with youth; how do they differ? Engage in what Love (2019) calls "intersectional justice," where we use texts that represent our students' complex identities while also engaging in conversations that can empower youth, by centering their voices and offering opportunities for literacy development, resistance, collaborations, and healing (p. 11).

In doing so, we must be vigilant about continually reflecting on our assumptions, and we must work daily on using discourse that does not generalize our conceptions of adolescence. When our discourse changes, so do our ideologies, dispositions, behaviors, and interactions with youth. In viewing adolescents from more open and complex perspectives, we can truly see their potential, intellect, creativity, and passions.

WHAT ARE THE THEORIES THAT GROUND BOOK CLUBS?

While this book centers students' voices, it is grounded in various pedagogical and psychological theories, which will be outlined throughout this book. Love (2019) explains that theory can be a place to explain "patterns of justice," to serve as a space for healing and to give us the "language to fight, the knowledge to stand on, and the humbling reality of what intersectional social justice is up against" (p. 132).

I ask you to imagine the liberatory and asset-based theories in this book as a chorus of voices that we will hear as we think through equitable practices within our book clubs. In later chapters, we will explore reader response theories, culturally affirming social-emotional learning, trauma-informed and healing-centered approaches, and critical literacy. For now, I will speak to two central theoretical approaches that will situate the framework and practices for this book: culturally sustaining approaches and bibliotherapy.

Culturally Sustaining Approaches

At the end of every academic year, I talk with students about their experiences with book clubs. Students reflect individually and collaboratively about what has been beneficial for them throughout the process. This questioning is a critical part of my development as a facilitator. Without a doubt, every year, students tell me that having choices in the books they read makes the book clubs more rewarding.

"I love that we can choose what we read in here," says Melody. "I love that I can connect to the characters and see pieces of me in the books we read."

Allowing for choice is just one aspect of the culturally sustaining approaches that will be modeled in this book. But it is not just our curriculum that must be culturally sustaining; our counseling and instructional strategies must also encompass this framework.

Theorists and practitioners of culturally sustaining pedagogy (CSP) define culture as a dynamic, evolving system that recognizes identities are not static—but are fluid and intersectional and include race, ethnicity, class, sexuality, gender, language, religion, immigration status, and youth culture (Ladson-Billings, 2014; Paris & Alim, 2014). Waitoller and King Thorius (2016) offer an extension to CSP, asking practitioners to also consider ability as an essential component of students' identities. Culturally sustaining facilitators must view our students' rich diversities as assets and strengths—and ultimately use these to select texts and build communities.

As culturally sustaining facilitators, we must also resist deficit approaches and instead work to sustain the "linguistic, literate, and cultural pluralism" of our students' identities and communities (Paris, 2012, p. 95). Paris and Alim (2014) remind us that culturally sustaining approaches must work to also de-center "White, middle-class, monolingual, and monocultural norms of educational achievement" to increase access and power for historically marginalized youth (p. 95).

Culturally sustaining approaches also demand that we develop and use critical methods to help our students confront, resist, and dismantle systemic oppression. Book clubs can be a powerful and intimate space where students speak to and reveal their own experiences with discrimination—and then collectively develop ways to counteract these aggressions. I will outline this process more richly in Chapter 6.

Most importantly, to create book clubs that are culturally sustaining, we want to maintain spaces that center love. Remember, the purpose of book clubs is to be inclusive and transformative. To create this environment, we need to develop and nurture processes that allow students to flourish. In the next section, we will see how bibliotherapy can help us achieve that loving stance with our students.

Bibliotherapy

The guidance counselor at my high school has graciously allowed me to borrow her office during lunchtime, and so I am crammed in this small space—built for five—but with eight 11th-grade female adolescents who have just finished reading *The Sisterhood of the Traveling Pants* (Brashares, 2003). After talking about how excited they are to see America Ferrera play Carmen's character, the young women discuss another character, Bridgette. They get fired up, irritated, and frustrated with her, who according to Keisha, has "thrown herself at Eric," her soccer coach. Gina agrees, shouting, "Right?! I wanted to hit her when she was at that bar!"

Julie concurs, "Yeah, she's a psycho."

Keisha continues, "She definitely needs to go to counseling."

"No, no, no!" yells Yoana, smiling broadly. "She needs to go to book club!"

The young women laugh and high-five, agreeing with Yoana's intervention advice.

This scene captures how young people can begin to equate book club with a space for healing. Grounded in research and practices of bibliotherapy, book clubs allow for processes where books can serve as catalysts for students to reflect on, understand, and negotiate their own social and emotional issues.

Coined by Samuel Crothers (1916), "bibliotherapy" is the use of texts to enhance social-emotional development. Practiced by librarians, teachers, psychologists, counselors, psychiatrists, and social workers, bibliotherapy can be used for intervention and prevention. Within school communities, social workers, counselors, psychiatrists, and psychologists can conduct *clinical bibliotherapy* as an intervention with psychotherapeutic methods.

Developmental bibliotherapy is more preventive and can be used by teachers, librarians, caregivers, and other school personnel to help youth in their personal growth.

Synonymous with bibliotherapy are reading therapy, book therapy, poetry therapy, and literary therapy. Put simply, bibliotherapy is the use of literature, film, or other types of multimedia to help adolescents deal with difficult life circumstances. When reading books in isolation, readers connect to the text; however, when reading *and* discussing books, the relationships become broader in that students begin to connect themselves and their experiences with their peers as well. Connecting youth to their peers can have a powerful impact and ultimately help enhance young people's social and emotional well-being (Elmore & Huebner, 2010).

Practitioners of bibliotherapy offer several stages of the process, the first being *identification*, where students see a character or situation within a text that mirrors their realities (Allen, Allen, Latrobe, Brand, Pfefferbaum, Elledge, Burton, & Guffey, 2012). Once students have identified a connection, they can experience a *catharsis*—which leads them to greater understandings of themselves and others. This then leads to *insight*, which we hope will ultimately motivate students to make changes within their lives. Another stage is *universalization*, where young people recognize they are not alone in their problems. Wilson and Thornton (2007/2008) describe an additional stage called *projection*, where readers consider what the text means for their futures.

Much research has evolved around bibliotherapy, suggesting that texts nurture emotional development, improve social and problem-solving skills, enhance self-concepts, and promote emotional intelligence (Forgan, 2002). Worldwide, practitioners of bibliotherapy have found that it helps young people deal with

- bullying (Duimstra, 2003);
- divorce, bereavement, and death (Corr, 2004; Pehrsson, Allen, Folger, McMillen, & Lowe, 2007);
- abuse and neglect (Betzalel & Shechtman, 2010; Foster, 2015);
- trauma and displacement (DeVries, Brennan, Lankin, Morse, Rix, & Beck, 2017; Rubio Cancino & Buitrago Cruz, 2019);
- identity development (Ford, Walters, & Byrd, 2019);
- anxiety, aggression, and depression (Cobham, 2012; Stice, Rohde, Gau, & Ochner, 2011); and
- coming out and other issues as related to LGBTQ youth (Frank & Cannon, 2009).

The research is clear—yet for many of our schools, unfortunately, the resources are low. Book clubs are cost-effective and only require a stack of books. Further, bibliotherapeutic book clubs that are conducted thoughtfully can be used in our communities by multiple educational and youth development professionals. This book will help you to hone your facilitative skills and promote spaces that build students' social-emotional, academic, and agentic capacities.

Later, I will discuss culturally affirming social-emotional learning and trauma-informed and healing-centered approaches (Ginwright, 2018; Simmons, 2019) so that facilitators who are not trained as counselors and social workers can deal with challenging topics that may arise within book clubs. As explained earlier, we cannot avoid discussion of trauma in our secondary classrooms. Up to two-thirds of U.S. children have experienced trauma—from abuse and neglect to witnessing or being survivors of natural disasters, violence, or displacement (Minahan, 2019). We also know that systemic racism and witnessing racialized violence continue to have adverse effects on the mental health of youth of color (Tynes, Willis, Stewart, & Hamilton, 2019). Within our classrooms, the histories and the literature we teach continue to be rife with pain and suffering, and yet, we often ignore ways in which our content can impact our students. My hope for this book is to peel back this curtain of denial—and help support facilitators with how we can deal with complex issues that will surface in our discussions. Trauma is unavoidable because we are humans, and we experience pain. These places of pain will undeniably intersect with our content.

The opening anecdote demonstrates this inevitability. The young women read about the death of the protagonist's father and instead of first exploring the imagery of the text, I asked students how they felt and connected to it. Most importantly, we created a space where we could empathize with one another's experiences. Thoughts of loss were triggered by the events in the book, because trauma lives in the content of our classrooms and our book clubs. But we can be more responsive, informed, and open about how students interact with that content and one another—and then use the human resources we have at our schools to support our students. This means working together as teachers and counselors, as administrators and paraprofessionals, as parent coordinators and speech pathologists, to ensure students' well-being. To avoid doing so is to ignore what gets in the way of our students experiencing success.

WHAT'S COMING UP?

This chapter elucidated what brings me to book club and the research and theories that ground and inform the narratives and suggestions. For the rest of the chapters, I will provide practical ways to facilitate these student-centered forums. Chapters 2, 3, and 4 provide the tools: How do we start book clubs? How do we create inclusive spaces that are student-centered? How can we become culturally sustaining facilitators? How do we maintain our book clubs? Each chapter will provide practical suggestions, with sample protocols, agendas, and activities to help you be successful and effective in your work.

Chapter 5 will do a deep dive into how book clubs can simultaneously address students' academic and social-emotional needs through careful selection of texts, targeted questioning, and facilitation techniques. Chapter 6 will share how book clubs can be used for critical conversations to build students' sense of advocacy and agency around social justice issues. Finally, Chapter 7 will strategize ways to involve our students' caregivers and families and tap into digital methods to engage students with texts and one another.

TAKE ACTION NOW!

I want to thank you for taking this journey with me. I hope by the end of our time together, you will see the power of book clubs within your communities and have solid plans for what book clubs will look like within your school context. Therefore, I encourage you to read this book with others. Perhaps you can create a book club within your community where this is your primary text. Think about the adults in your building, your collaborators, who might be interested in engaging in and advancing literacies, culturally affirming social-emotional learning, and social justice.

Perhaps it is your social studies, science, or English department working alongside instructional coaches, or it is your grade-level team. Perhaps you are a social worker, speech pathologist, or counselor, and you want to read this text with another teacher so that you can work together to create book clubs. Perhaps you are a preservice teacher or counselor in methods classes, and you are reading this book in a group to think about how your future approaches will look as you enter school and community-based spaces. Or, maybe you are reading this book on your own, thinking about ways you can do the work in your context and collaborate with others in the upcoming months.

Regardless of your positionality or context, grab a highlighter or pen, a stack of sticky notes, or a journal to log your ideas. Engage with this text critically, continually keeping your contexts and communities in mind. I will undoubtedly share stories and offer suggestions that might *not* work for you, but take the nuggets that *will* work—and modify those that *could* work. The key is to imagine spaces of joy, healing, resistance, collaboration, and justice—and begin planning methods to create and sustain book clubs in thoughtful and intentional ways. I ask that before you do that, however, you also begin to reflect on who you are and where you come from—as our identities and life stories will impact how we interact with youth. Thus, I've offered a reflective planning template to use throughout the book. In addition, I have a website, educateforaction.com, which provides a plethora of resources. I will refer to this site frequently (as simply "the website"), and it will become an important supplementary tool as you can download files and modify them as necessary. The first resource you will find will be the full blank planning template. I ask that before moving on to Chapter 2 you fill out these opening portions of the template to think deeply about how and why you come to this work.

Self-Reflection
Who are you?   • What are the identities and intersectionalities that make *you* who *you* are? You might consider race, ethnicity, language, ability, gender, sexuality, religion, and immigrant and socioeconomic status.   • What are your interests and hobbies? What brings you joy?
Describe your own literacies as an adolescent.   • As an adolescent, did you like to read and write? What were your motivations and dispositions?   • What kinds of things did you read and write? What types of literacies did you engage in (i.e., social media, hip-hop, poetry)? When and where did your literacies happen (i.e., at home, in coffee shops, with friends)?   • In what ways did you engage in your school communities? Where and when did you participate the most? The least?
Describe your literacies now.   • Do you like to read and write now? What are your current motivations and dispositions?   • What kinds of things do you read and write? When and where do your literacies happen? What types of literacies do you engage in?   • In what ways do you currently engage in your school communities? Where and when do you participate the most? The least?

QR Code for the Supplementary Website

CHAPTER 2

Getting Book Clubs Started Within Our School Communities

Today I am visiting Shahnaj, one of my graduate students in the literacy program at Hunter College. She has decided to focus her thesis on book clubs and has asked me to provide her with feedback, as part of her practicum. Today will be her first day of facilitating book clubs in her 10th-grade classroom located in a public school in the South Bronx.

When I arrive, I am not surprised by the metal detectors nor the barrage of security guards and policing methods that continue to infiltrate our school communities. Yet when I walk into Shahnaj's classroom, I am immediately transported to a space of tranquility and openness. Her desks are grouped by fours, with each quad covered with a red and white checkered tablecloth with fake candles and flowers. Jazz plays in the background while Shahnaj passes out book club "menus" and five different texts to each table. Projected on her whiteboard is a sign that reads Sultana's Starbooks Café.

When the bell rings, I find a solitary desk in the corner. Shahnaj's students, all Latinx adolescents, come in lively and happy to see her. They "ooh" and "aah" over the classroom transformation and find their seats. Shahnaj explains that they are going to participate in a "book tasting," where students will sample from such texts as *Finding Miracles* (Alvarez, 2006), *Of Beetles and Angels* (Asgedom, 2002), *A Long Way Gone* (Beah, 2008), *Enrique's Journey* (Nazario, 2007), and *When I Was a Puerto Rican* (Santiago, 2006).

Shahnaj asks students to open their menus and tells them that they will travel to different tables to try another "course"—or book. She gives them 10 minutes to peruse the books at each station and asks them to write their initial thoughts of the texts (see the website for Shahnaj's notetaker). As students travel around the room, Shahnaj sits with them, answering questions about the books. When they are done, she asks them what the books have in common. Several students around the room raise their hands. Shahnaj nods to one young man, sitting at the back table.

"Immigration," he says proudly, and Shahnaj thanks him for his contribution. She explains that students will be in small groups this month, with each group reading a different narrative about immigration. She shares how eager she is for the books, and the students concur. I hear many of them whispering how "good" the texts look. One student shouts from the corner, "I really want to read *A Long Way Gone*, Miss!"

Shahnaj smiles, replying, "I am so happy to see how excited you are! And I will try my best to give you your first or second choices. On the back of your menu, can you please tell me what those are? Tomorrow, I will surprise you with your favorite meal!"

The students begin whispering at their tables again, writing in their choices, with some looking across the room at their friends to see what they are choosing. The class reverberates with energy and enthusiasm. And I can't help but think that it is because of Shahnaj's efforts and disposition and, of course, the magic of book clubs.

WHO CAN START AND FACILITATE BOOK CLUBS?

The answer here is anyone! Shahnaj provides us with just one example of a potential facilitator: the teacher. Although book clubs are primarily led by the students, teachers start the book club process and then serve as facilitators, traveling from group to group, offering support and guidance. But this book is not just for teachers—nor is it just for classroom practices. Book clubs can be started and facilitated by multiple school personnel for different purposes.

Before beginning our book clubs, we need to always think about our purpose. Let's return to Shahnaj. Her purposes for book clubs were threefold: to enhance students' understanding and perspectives in issues pertaining to immigration, to build students' reading comprehension and levels of textual analysis, and to increase students' discussion skills. These are all academic purposes for book clubs. However, Shahnaj also wanted to use book clubs for developmental bibliotherapeutic purposes. Many of her students are recent immigrants or children of immigrants. Shahnaj selected these texts intentionally so that students could experience social-emotional growth by making connections with the characters and the writers. In doing so, students can grapple with a myriad of issues, including dual identities of their U.S. cultures and their homelands and challenges of integrating into a new country. While Shahnaj focuses on students' literacy growth, the book clubs also serve as a place for students to forge connections with the books and one another through the texts and conversations.

These spaces are not just reserved for the classroom, however. School personnel such as administrators, parent coordinators, speech pathologists, and librarians can also facilitate developmental bibliotherapeutic book clubs. Worldwide, librarians hold a variety of book clubs in their libraries with the purposes of engaging students with literature and connecting texts to their lives. Kunzel and Hardesty (2006), for example, have written a comprehensive guide for how to create teen-centered book clubs within our libraries. Research has demonstrated that librarians can successfully provide developmental bibliotherapy by offering books that match readers' needs or facilitating book clubs. Tukhareli (2011), as another example, studied bibliotherapeutic book clubs in South Africa with youth diagnosed with HIV, finding that book clubs were an effective way of getting young people connected around a common need. In this scenario, adolescents not only learned more about their diagnosis, but they reported they had a decreased level of fear and increased comfort level in talking about their health.

Libraries can be safe spaces for youth, where readers can select books and connect with other students who have similar concerns. Further, librarians can work with teachers, counselors, and social workers to identify texts that might serve as bibliotherapy. Thus, book clubs can also be held either in the classrooms or in the library, with the librarian and teacher or the librarian and social worker co-facilitating groups. In Scotland, local librarians partnered with mental health professionals, creating a program called "Read Yourself Well" (MacDonald, Vallance, & McGrath, 2012). The librarians highlighted books that could serve as bibliotherapeutic texts while the mental health professionals were available to hold sessions with readers about making decisions for texts and using them for therapeutic purposes.

Administrators can also take a lead role in facilitating book clubs. Mark Federman, a principal in New York City, runs book clubs for his students, keeping an extensive young adult library in his office (Booth & Rowsell, 2006). Over the years, he has developed and refined the "Principal's Book Club," visiting classrooms to give book talks and facilitating small groups of students who talk about issues from racism and homophobia to peer pressure and relationships. Not only can administrators build strong relationships with their students, but they can also model how to build community and offer supportive spaces for literacy growth and social-emotional learning.

Counselors, school psychologists, psychiatrists, and social workers may also want to facilitate book clubs, perhaps using clinical bibliotherapy, where they lead groups around more challenging issues that require counseling knowledge and skills. Book clubs can thus be organized around various topics, from abuse or trauma to depression or anxiety. Like group therapy, students can connect and share experiences so that they realize they are not living in isolation. The books serve as supplemental therapeutic tools in that students may feel reticent or afraid to voice their feelings and reveal their own experiences. In discussing the characters first, students can talk about emotions and behaviors without telling their stories. Ultimately, the books become catalysts where students use texts as springboards to share their own concerns.

WHAT IS THE PURPOSE OF YOUR BOOK CLUBS AND WHO WILL PARTICIPATE?

We've seen that book clubs can be facilitated by a range of people within our communities. Let's look deeper now into our purposes for book clubs, which we need to consider intentionally before beginning. English teachers, for example, might focus on building students' analytical reading skills, while science or social studies teachers might focus on deepening students' understanding of their content. On the other hand, counselors or social workers might focus on perhaps addressing trauma or helping students transition from middle to high school. Concretizing your purpose for book clubs is critical since before we begin, we want to be thoughtful of who we are working with and what we want to achieve.

Sometimes, however, the purpose of book clubs depends on our students. For example, one of my out-of-classroom book clubs was a group of 12 young women who just wanted to read books by and for women in a collective space. The purpose of our book club was broader: to use texts and each other to deal with issues as they arose in the books and connected to the young women's lives. Ultimately, the students decided both the books we read and the topics we discussed. We read everything from *Like Sisters on the Homefront* (Williams-Garcia, 1998) to *The Coldest Winter Ever* (Souljah, 2005). The luxury of out-of-classroom book clubs is that there are no curriculum constraints or mandated texts, and we have much more flexibility and freedom for students to select books and topics.

The primary goal is to think first about who our students are and their corresponding needs. These two processes should inform one another. If you are a teacher facilitating book clubs in your classroom, you should further consider your curriculum demands and how you can balance this content with students' cultures and interests. In returning to Shahnaj, she knew she had to teach particular literacy strategies—but she could do so by using culturally sustaining texts that centered students' experiences.

WHERE AND WHEN DO WE MEET?

Once we've established our purpose for book clubs, we should reflect on the nuts and bolts of where and when our book clubs will take place. If we are teachers, we might consider using book clubs as part of our instructional process within our classroom spaces. However, if we conduct book clubs outside of structured class time, we need to find and negotiate new spaces, which can be difficult for teachers and other school personnel. When I was a teacher and facilitated book clubs outside of class as an extracurricular activity, I couldn't use my own classroom because it was used for tutoring during lunch and after school.

So, sometimes, we have to get creative. Book clubs, for example, can be held in counselors' or principals' offices or libraries. The key is to find spaces that are quiet and where we won't be interrupted. Often young people share sensitive information, and we don't want folks to barge in during this time of release and connection. I recommend putting a sign on the door asking people to not disturb the group unless it is an emergency.

If school spaces aren't possible, we might look within our school's community. One year, a local coffee shop gave me their basement seating area for 30 minutes every Friday after school. Local libraries and bookstores are other good resources for space as they want to encourage adolescents and their reading. When the weather is nice, head to the park with a blanket and snacks. It might not be as quiet or as private—but it's important to be creative and flexible when facilitating book clubs. A bonus is that these outside spaces can allow students to experience connection with you and one another within a new context. Just be sure to follow the appropriate protocol for meeting with students off-campus; caregivers and families should know where their children are.

Timing is also essential to consider. In terms of conducting in-class book clubs, as a classroom teacher, I have found that doing them later in the school year has been helpful since this delay allows me to build students' literacy skills and develop our classroom community. For example, I can teach and model how to use various reading strategies such as visualize, make connections, summarize, and analyze with our shared texts so that students are more successful in doing this work in groups on a more independent level. Waiting until later in the year to start book clubs also allows students to build relationships with one another. These first few months are critical for us to get to know one another and to learn how to engage in small-group conversations.

If I am conducting book clubs outside of classrooms, where our central goals may not be directly related to literacy development, I usually start in September so that we have the entire school year to build deep relationships. In the past, I have conducted these sessions during lunch or after school. However, if school counselors, psychologists, and social workers already have group therapy sessions during the school day, book clubs can be conducted during these times.

As to how long and how often clubs should meet, this depends on the context of your school and your book club. For teachers, the timing will vary depending on whether you have shorter periods or longer blocks. In my previous high school, I taught on a modified block with 250 minutes of instruction per week. In this case, students read independently three times a week (20 minutes on Mondays, Wednesdays, and Fridays). Our book clubs then met every Friday for 30 minutes total. Depending on your student population, these opportunities can be shorter in the beginning stages and gradually become longer over time to build students' stamina in reading and participating in student-led conversations. A sample schedule is offered on the website.

For my out-of-classroom book clubs, we met once per week for 45–60 minutes, depending on the time of day. For some groups, we met at lunch, so we had only 45 minutes. For other groups, we met after school, so we had much more flexibility, but in general, students stayed for about an hour.

As for keeping the momentum, for out-of-classroom book clubs, we met for an entire year—and for those 9th-grade young women in Chapter 1, we met for 4 years, throughout their time in high school. If you are a teacher, though, conducting in-class book clubs, curriculum constraints may limit you to one or two marking periods per year, depending on the grade level of your students.

Take a look at the following planning template. Use this space to begin planning your own book clubs. First, and most importantly, consider why you are starting book clubs and who your audience is. Think deeply about your student population and consider their cultural and linguistic diversities, abilities, interests, and needs. This means becoming a "student of your students," which can be done by building relationships with them, asking them questions, and surveying them to get to know and understand their lived experiences, backgrounds, identities, and interests. Next, we need to think about the purposes and goals of our book clubs. Based on your student population, what best fits the needs and interests of your students? And will those goals be decided by you or collaboratively with your students? Finally, think practically: Where and when will they take place—and for how long?

Pre-Planning for Book Clubs
Describe your student population. Consider students' identities, communities, cultural and linguistic diversities, abilities, interests, and needs.
What are the purposes or goals of your book clubs? (Based on your student population and the context of your book club/s, what goals best fit the needs and interests of your students? Will the goals be decided by you or in collaboration with your students?)
Where and when will your book clubs take place? (What space seems most conducive for book clubs? What months will you begin and end book clubs? What time of the day will they occur? How often and for how long?)

WHICH BOOKS DO WE USE AND HOW DO WE GET THEM?

Once you've set a time and location for your book clubs, the next step is selecting your texts. The first year I facilitated book clubs, this was no easy task. Enthusiastic to bring book clubs into my classroom, I visited my principal for book monies. Unfortunately, there were none to be had. Not ready to give up, I went to my greatest resource: the school librarian.

At the time, I taught two sections of "Intensive Reading," which were for juniors and seniors who had not passed our state-mandated reading test. Students and I began our work together in August and, in March, they took the test. For 7 months, I helped prepare them for this test in ways I hoped were culturally responsive and sustaining.

But, I must admit, the freedom that came after that test was liberating! And so one week before the impending exam, I spent a lovely Friday afternoon perusing bookshelves, with one basic requirement: Do you have three or more copies of a text? At first our librarian went to canonical books, *The Catcher in the Rye* and *Fahrenheit 451*. Knowing that my students would encounter these books in their English classes—and considering how I suffered through them in my own high school career—I opted for contemporary young adult literature that reflected my students' cultural and linguistic diversities and reading levels.

Our librarian was a magician; she found copies of such texts as *Slam!* (Myers, 1996), *Romiette and Julio* (Draper, 2001), *The Last Vampire* (Pike, 1994), and *Trino's Choice* (Bertrand, 1999). My classes consisted of mostly boys, many of whom were recent immigrants from Cuba and Haiti. My purposes in the book clubs were to generate more student-led, authentic discussions and enhance their appreciation for reading. Therefore, I selected books that were available, of course, and that, most importantly, reflected their identities, communities, and interests.

Many students, unfortunately, told me they did not like reading. And who could blame them? For many, they had been pushed into remedial courses that focused on skill-and-drill worksheets, and I wanted to get as far away as possible from those kinds of practices.

While the first session of our book clubs was far from perfect (as is always the case when we do something new), the energy and enthusiasm of our 3 months together were enough for me to change how I structured my future classes. Students were empowered by choosing what they read and discussed. And they devoured the books.

For example, high school senior Freddie, who called himself the "Haitian Sensation," led an all-boys book club, where the young men opted to read not just the first book in *The Last Vampire* series, but all three. I was both surprised by their choice in text and inspired by their conversations. Never having read the book myself, I thought they would talk about the macabre. Yet, the young men made powerful connections to the text and to one another, discussing such issues as rituals and beliefs, their home countries, the deaths of family members and friends, and love. I often would walk by Freddie's group and see him looking intently at his peers as they spoke, nodding his head and repeating, "That is deep, man. That is deep."

Serving as both teacher and coach in urban and low socioeconomic areas for the past 25 years, I have experienced the financial realities and disparities within our school systems; I also realize that some schools may not even have the privilege of a library within their communities. However, resources do exist.

That following year, I went to the Parent-Teacher Association, and they granted me $300 for books. Another year, I wrote a small grant through Donors Choose, a nonprofit agency that publicizes teachers' needs on their website so that outside funders can contribute. I also went from garage and yard sales in Florida to, in later years, stoop sales in Brooklyn, purchasing books for less than a dollar. Other great resources for free books are local libraries, where staff often clean out their spaces and give away texts to teachers.

We must also think outside of the "book." Graphic novels, comic books, and manga are wonderful options for students, as are digital books. In addition, some students prefer to read on their phones or tablets, and public libraries offer audio and digital texts for free. Sites such as bookbub.com also provide discounted digital books every week.

I'll certainly never say the work of book club is easy—but the rewards make these resourceful efforts worth the time and energy.

When purchasing texts, it is also important that we be thoughtful about our selections. For me, I was initially limited by resources. However, in the following years, I could be much more intentional with the choice of texts and allow students to help me make those decisions. For example, when I conducted book clubs outside of the classroom, we took visits to our school library—and even local bookstores—where students could peruse the shelves and talk to one another about the kinds of texts they wanted to read. I also recycle book club texts from previous years and have my students choose from those.

In selecting texts, we want to be mindful of our students, their cultural and linguistic diversities, abilities, and interests. It's also important to be mindful of the purpose of our book clubs. While I always offer culturally relevant texts for my students, it's critical to interrogate what constitutes culture. Saldana (2020) argues that culture is not just about "race or ethnicity, heritage language, and place of origin" (p. 51), but also includes adolescents' lived experiences as adolescents are "complex and complicated beings in need of a similarly complex and complicated literature that reflects them more fully" (p. 52). Again, in making it a priority to get to know our students and build relationships with them, our selections for texts will improve so that they can connect and engage with the reading and one another.

Often teachers ask me if they should also consider books based on students' reading levels. When I think of this question, I am brought to an experience in my personal life when my younger brother, Patrick, came home from middle school one day. He said he was excited to be part of a book club and to read the book *Hatchet* (Paulsen, 2006) but that his teacher said he couldn't, because it was above his reading level. Instead, he got placed into another group with a book he was not interested in. Not only was he reading something he did not like, but he also now associated his reading identity with inadequacy.

Hoffman (2017) warns us that there are many unintended consequences of leveling readers and texts. As evidenced with Patrick, youth can begin associating their reading identities with their reading levels, perpetuating low self-esteem. Reading levels also feed into deficit discourses, as we begin to equate low reading levels with such words as *struggling, poor, low,* or *reluctant* (Frankel & Brooks, 2018). I wonder if Patrick would be reading more now if his teacher had told him he was developing as a reader—or that he was a reader who excelled with informational texts. Or perhaps she could have provided him with the audio version of the book—or reached out to his family, offering us the opportunity to support him at home.

When we focus solely on leveling books and readers, we ignore our students' backgrounds and experiential knowledge. Let's say I have a student who reads at a 900 Lexile, and he wants to read a book about skateboarding but the book is at an 1100 Lexile. I'm not going to deny him this opportunity as Patrick's teacher did. This student has been skating for years! He comes to the text with a ton of background knowledge for him to experience success. Now, if I were to give him a book about say, cabinet-making, written at an 1100 Lexile, yes, he might struggle. I would struggle with that book— because I know nothing about cabinet-making! Later in this book, we will talk extensively about how to help students with more challenging texts. The point here, though, is that we need to look at our students as having complex reading identities that cannot be measured just with numbers. Further, like our students' identities, we must remember that their reading abilities are not "static"—that we *all* experience joyous and successful experiences, just like we *all* also experience struggle with demanding texts (Frankel & Brooks, 2018).

We also don't want to use these Lexile levels to gauge our students' success in reading. Think about your own experiences as a developing reader— or even now as a reader. As an adolescent, I was proud when I finished all the books by a particular author or when I spent an entire Sunday afternoon reading for pleasure. Success in reading should not just be associated with test scores, but the myriad of ways in which readers can achieve growth by developing their preferences, dispositions, fluencies, persistence, levels of experimentation and openness, and abilities to talk about texts. As facilitators, we must remember to engage in the reading processes in humanizing ways, building on students' assets and their cultural, linguistic, literacy, and experiential resources (Frankel & Brooks, 2018).

I know this may read a bit "pie in the sky." And I will be honest: I struggle with the issue still. At my previous high school, we measured students'

Lexile levels three times a year, in September, January, and June—to document their growth. I used those numbers to differentiate texts in our content-area classrooms. When I co-taught science with Theresa, on Fridays, we facilitated "article clubs," where we would access leveled texts from Newsela .com. All of our students read about the same content (i.e., pollution), but different students received different texts based on their reading levels so that they could experience success with the content.

Within my English Language Arts (ELA) classes, I had a different approach, allowing students to choose their independent reading books. While we did discuss the "levels" of books, I also talked with them about the font size: Is it too small? The size of the book: Does it feel too big and dense? The content: Do I enjoy or connect to what the book is about?

Then I'd ask them to read the first page. Does it grab you? As you read, did you use the five-finger rule? Were there more than five words on that first page you didn't know? If so, maybe that book might be too hard.

Sometimes I had students who did not want to "challenge" themselves. My former student Joe read all of the *Diary of a Wimpy Kid* (Kinney, 2007) books in the 10th grade. He told me, "I know these are too easy. But I like them. They make me laugh. And I hate reading."

So I met Joe where he was. Later, once we established a trusting relationship, I introduced him to more challenging books with humor such as *Bucking the Sarge* (Curtis, 2006), *The Absolutely True Diary of a Part-Time Indian* (Alexie, 2009), and *Spanking Shakespeare* (Wizner, 2008).

During our shared reading time, when we read books as a whole class, I could also challenge students, but with support. Together, we read *The Bluest Eye* (Morrison, 2007) and *The Brief Wondrous Life of Oscar Wao* (Diaz, 2008). And I could sleep at night because I knew that students could read what they wanted—while also experiencing supported, culturally relevant reading challenges as a whole class.

My biggest takeaway here is to allow for choice. If students do not enjoy or connect with the texts we provide, then book clubs will not engage our students. Therefore, it is paramount that we continually listen to them and integrate their interests, cultures, and lived experiences into our rationales for text selections.

As one last example that reflects the importance of choice, in 2019, I worked in a special education school where most of our students were diagnosed with autism. Therefore, I picked books where the main characters or authors also had autism. My purposes were to increase students' dispositions for reading and to acknowledge and celebrate neurodiversity, while also helping students deal with some of the challenges of autism. Students could choose from such texts as *On the Edge of Gone* (Duyvis, 2016), *Episodes: Scenes from Life, Love, and Autism* (Ginsberg, 2012), *Atypical: Life With Asperger's in 20 ⅓ Chapters* (Saperstein, 2010), or *Marcelo in the Real World* (Stork, 2011).

On the day we looked through the books, I approached Khalid about what he wanted to read. His response was "This is stupid. Reading is dumb, and these books suck."

I was a bit stunned. Why wouldn't Khalid and others want to read books that might reflect their neurodiversities? But for Khalid—and Kayla and Russell—they did not want to read about autism. I made a dangerous assumption about what books they wanted to read. And so I went back to the drawing board *with* them and asked, "What do you like to read?"

Khalid answered candidly, "Nothing. Ever. I hate it."

"Okay," I said. "I get it. What kinds of shows do you watch? Do you like movies? What are your interests? Let's talk and get to know each other better."

The four of us discussed these questions, and I found they all liked science fiction, with Khalid enjoying movies with war motifs. I came back the next week with a stack of books based on their interests, and they ended up selecting *We See Everything* (Sutcliffe, 2017), a postapocalyptic story about two young men who were impacted by drone wars.

Did we talk about autism during our book clubs? Sometimes. We always began our sessions discussing our lives and connecting—and autism came up. But as I learned from Kayla, not all students want to read about what is troubling them, or about their identities, or their sexualities or abilities. Kayla read to escape, explaining, "I read to get away from autism. We always talk about our autism here, at school, at home. I'm sick of talking about autism." And so we didn't. But we still read, even Khalid, and we had many powerful conversations.

Again, the idea is to be flexible—and to listen to students to find out what they need. It also means getting to know books—and not just those of the canon. Some of you may be English teachers, and you may want to focus on those canonical texts in your book clubs, especially if, for example, you are teaching Advanced Placement (AP) English, which has a long required book list. Why not allow students to choose from this list based on their own identities, experiences, and interests?

HOW CAN WE BE MORE INTENTIONAL ABOUT THE BOOKS WE READ?

As was stated previously, we must always consider our purpose before starting book clubs. This purpose will then become a critical way for us to be intentional about our text selection. For me, I come to book clubs with the dual purpose of enhancing academic and social-emotional learning, so I have found contemporary young adult literature (YAL) to be the most impactful in meeting both of these purposes. Research demonstrates that because YAL connects to youth experiences, it can help adolescents build relationships, enhance their intellect and social-emotional literacies, and develop their sense of agency (Ivey & Johnston, 2013; Riesco, 2021). Further, YAL provides a space "for the exploration and development of more liberating identities" (Glenn & Ginsberg, 2016, p. 94), giving youth opportunities to discover questions and issues that matter most to them. Much YAL also allows students to explore sociopolitical issues, helping them to understand themselves and their roles within contemporary contexts (Ivey & Johnston, 2017; Riesco, 2021).

We should, however, if choosing to use YAL, select texts with a critical eye and mind, and ask ourselves the following questions:

- Do these texts match the linguistic and cultural diversities of my students?
- Do they consider their variety of abilities?
- Do they represent or address their needs, interests, and identities?
- Do they reinforce stereotypes based on the characters' race, ethnicities, gender, class, abilities, languages, or sexualities?
- Do they reinforce any stereotypical views of youth?

Let's press into this last question. Scholars in the field of adolescence ask us to critically look at how youth are represented in books (Lewis & Petrone, 2010; Sarigianides, 2012). Remember in the last chapter when we explored the complexities of young adults? Well, we want our books to represent those complexities too. Perhaps, then, consider facilitating book clubs where your purpose is to have students deconstruct how youth are portrayed in the texts.

Sulzer and Thein (2016) offer us engaging questions that youth and teachers can use to think about ways youth are portrayed:

- To what extent do portrayals of adolescents in the story align with common understandings about adolescents' needs, desires, and abilities? To what extent do the portrayals of adolescents raise questions about what is "normal"?
- In what ways do young people's intersectional identities inform the progression of the story? How do these intersectional identities complicate common understandings about how youth fit into society?
- What situations, actions, or pieces of dialogue does the author use to mark a character as being an adolescent? How is adolescence as a social construct leveraged in these textual elements?
- In what ways does the narrative voice evoke ideas of adolescents? How is this voice in conversation with various beliefs about the place of youth in society?

The website includes suggestions for specific titles of contemporary and young adult books, organized thematically to address various issues. Further,

I provide various websites, including resources for integrating social justice issues, locating diverse texts, and acquiring funding for books.

HOW DO WE GET STUDENTS TO JOIN BOOK CLUBS?

Now that we've deeply considered our purposes and our text selections, our next step is to think about getting students involved. In 2005, I recruited students for my first school-based, out-of-class book clubs. As a literacy coach, I knew all the ELA teachers and asked each of them if I could borrow 5 to 10 minutes at the end of class to promote book club. Mostly my script included when we would meet (after school or during lunch) and what we would do (discuss books and how they connect to our lives). I also brought copies of young adult books so that students could get a sense of the kinds of texts we would read. I did clarify, however, that they would ultimately select the books—and that these were just examples of some books we could read together.

I also gave students informational flyers with my name, room number, and email address (see the website for a sample). These flyers were posted throughout the school as well. I asked students to sign the flyer and provide their email address if they were interested so I could follow up with them. The flyers also provided dates for two informational meetings, which were held once during lunch and once after school.

I held the informational meetings in a classroom for about 45 minutes, the length of a book club. During this time, students filled out profile sheets so I could get to know them better (see the website for a sample). I also asked them to introduce themselves, to share their names, their favorite books or genres, and the reasons why they were interested in book club. We then perused and discussed the books that I brought.

HOW DO WE BUILD COMMUNITY TO PREPARE STUDENTS FOR CLASSROOM-BASED BOOK CLUBS?

Now that we've discussed recruitment strategies for out-of-classroom book clubs, let's focus on our classroom-based book clubs and how we can get them started. The most critical first step is getting to know our students—and having them get to know one another. Think about community-building activities that have been effective for you in your teaching experiences—or think about community-building activities you have experienced as an adolescent or adult that have been effective in helping you to get to know your peers. These experiences should be meaningful—and students should understand the purpose of such activities. So be explicit. Tell them why they are participating in these engagements. You might share research that demonstrates when students feel safe and part of a community, the learning becomes easier—and our cognitive processes are enhanced (Côté-Lussier & Fitzpatrick, 2016; Willis, 2017).

For me, my favorite opening activities are collaborative and creative. For example, during our first week together, we do a "speed meeting" activity, where students interview each other. Students develop the questions on our first day, and I collect them. I then use these questions to create a graphic organizer. The next day, students talk to three other students in class and take notes on their organizers (see the website for a sample). They ask questions back and forth, listen to each other, and record their peers' thoughts and ideas. Students then write up a paragraph explaining what they learned about others, and these paragraphs are later shared with three new students so that we all begin to get to know one another better.

I also ask my students to create "life maps" where they sketch out and write about what makes up their identities and communities. I also show them my life map so that they can get to know me too (see the website for a sample). Students can choose to include any of the following aspects of themselves (and more): name, race/ethnicity, gender, abilities, sexuality, languages, neighborhood, beliefs, schooling experiences, passions, communities, families, and interests. When they are done, students then meet in small groups to discuss their shared commonalities. If students feel comfortable, we hang these inside our classroom.

While I use these activities as a classroom teacher, they can also be offered in our out-of-classroom book clubs. On the first day you meet with students, for example, have them create life maps, if that feels appropriate. Regardless what you choose, it's important to engage in these activities so that students get to know one another and begin building trust and authentic relationships.

HOW DO WE BUILD LITERACY SKILLS TO PREPARE STUDENTS FOR CLASSROOM-BASED BOOK CLUBS?

In addition to building community within classroom spaces, I build students' literacy skills before beginning my in-class book clubs. This means that with our culturally relevant shared texts, we practice how to read them critically. During my first quarter of the school year, for example, I often start with *The Brief Wondrous Life of Oscar Wao* (Diaz, 2008), as most of my classes have consisted of primarily Latinx adolescents from the Dominican Republic. In reading this novel, students learn a variety of reading strategies, including how to make predictions and personal connections, how to write summaries, how to ask questions, and how to analyze. Students spend time on each of these skills, with me modeling and students practicing both with a partner and independently. If I facilitate out-of-classroom book clubs, this scaffolding can be done as well, where I model for youth how to respond and use various reading strategies. We will go over this instruction in much more depth in Chapter 5, where I provide specific examples of teaching these skills.

For my in-class book clubs, I also help prepare students by developing their discussion skills using the fishbowl method. A *fishbowl* is when the class is divided into two groups, where one group sits in an outside circle and another group sits in an inside circle so that the outside group can observe and reflect on the conversations of the inside group. To prepare for fishbowl, throughout the week my students "collect" significant passages, connections, and questions from our shared text (see Figure 2.1). These are kept in their reading journals or on graphic organizers.

I also model for students how I decide what is significant in my reading and how I might analyze that passage. I model how to make a variety of personal connections, including text-to-self, text-to-world, and text-to-text, and I teach students different kinds of questions they can pose to their peers, including clarifying, inferential, and applied questions. For each skill, I might spend a week of deep practice; this could look like introducing the skill on a Monday and modeling it every day of the week. Students then practice that skill with a small group or partner and independently. I move on to a new skill when I feel like most of the students can accomplish that reading strategy and then meet with students through guided reading or afterschool tutoring if they need additional support.

On Fridays, students come to class prepared for our fishbowl, where half the class sits in an outer circle and the other half sits in the inner circle. Students are paired up, with Partner A in the inner circle and Partner B in the outer circle. The inner circle brings their notes to discuss whereas the outer circle takes notes on the conversations and gives their partner feedback on their participation (see the website for a sample). These students talk for 15 minutes and then all the Partner Bs switch with Partner As so that the roles are reversed. I also always keep one empty chair in the inner circle, in case anyone in the outer circle has something to share that they just can't keep in.

Figure 2.1. Note-Taking Graphic Organizer

My Favorite Passages	My Questions
My Connections to the Text	My Thinking as I Read

This kind of scaffolding helps students develop their conversational skills, which are needed for book clubs. But these skills don't happen miraculously on their own. We collaboratively create agreements for our conversations and then hang those on chart paper to remember (see the website for samples). I also provide sentence starters to help students develop language for our conversations. We talk explicitly about both our verbal and body language, because how we are positioned sometimes demonstrates to others how engaged we are.

For the first fishbowl session, I interrupt a lot—not to be annoying—but to talk explicitly about discussion behaviors I notice. During one class session, for example, I asked my students to "Freeze. What do we notice about Juan's body language right now?"

Julia said, "He's looking at the person who is talking and nodding his head."

"Exactly," I responded. "And what does that tell Maria, who is talking?"

"That he's listening," Donald explained.

Sometimes I give students hidden "roles" during this initial session, where they act out behaviors that might happen. For example, with the inner circle, I'll give index cards that read:

- You will demonstrate someone who dominates the conversation.
- You will be very quiet and not talk.
- You dislike the book.
- You are very thoughtful of others.

Students take on (or act out) these roles for just 10 minutes or so. And just like the previous "freezing" exercise, I stop students and have them notice different kinds of behaviors. During one class, I asked, "What do you notice about David right now?"

"He's talking too much and not giving others time to say anything," said Jasmine.

"And how does that impact the group?"

"It doesn't give anyone time to speak," Jasmine continued.

"So what could David do? What are some strategies he could consider?"

We then discussed how to be reflective of our own space in conversations. We also strategized what we could do to intervene and disrupt this kind of participation. For example, a student might say, "David, while we appreciate your comments, I think it's time that we hear from some other voices."

And again, while this was done in my classroom space as an educator, this process can easily be replicated for our out-of-classroom book clubs as well. Provide students with the role index cards mentioned above and give them time to negotiate how to grapple with some of the challenges they may face during group conversations.

Throughout this book, I will offer many more of these kinds of scaffolding opportunities that we can use both in and out of class, as we help students to develop their literacy and social skills. For now, let's stop and do some reflecting on getting our book clubs started.

Based on your student population, what kinds of books and/or themes do you want to address in your book clubs?

OUT OF CLASS BOOK CLUBS: Recruitment Strategies
What recruitment strategies will you use?

What are some ways you can build community in your classroom and/or in your book clubs? How will you get to know your students? How will they get to know you? How will they get to know each other?	What are some ways to scaffold students' literacy and social skills?	
	How might you prepare students for reading strategies they will need to be successful in book clubs?	How might you prepare students for discussion strategies they will need to be successful in book clubs?

TAKE ACTION NOW!

Whether you are reading this book for a methods class, for your school community book club, or on your own, let's plan for action!

☐ Find your collaborators. Who will hold you accountable? Who can you have supportive conversations with—yet who will also challenge you? Find those people and share your ideas for book clubs. If you are a teacher, librarian, parent coordinator, or administrator, for example, talk to your social worker and get some advice about how to lead group discussions. Talk to the experts at your school about trauma-informed, healing-centered, and culturally affirming approaches to social-emotional learning (Ginwright, 2018; Simmons, 2019). And if you are a social worker or counselor, talk to your literacy coach, your reading specialist, or your librarian about great books for adolescents—or talk to them about ways you can support students' literacies.

☐ Begin to explore space in your school community. What makes sense for your context and your students?

☐ Read, listen, and ask! Peruse the website for recommendations for texts and resources. Also, ask students and colleagues about great books for youth that center diverse adolescent experiences. Then start reading—or listening to those texts. (I listen to audiobooks while taking a walk or cooking dinner. Audio File at www .audiofilemagazine.com/sync, as an example, offers dozens of free young adult books every summer.) Become familiar with all the terrific texts out there!

☐ If you are conducting out-of-class book clubs, develop an engaging, eye-catching flyer.

☐ Develop surveys and creative assignments and activities for getting to know your students better.

QR Code for Chapter 2 Resources

Creating Student-Centered, Inclusive Spaces Through Culturally Sustaining and Emotionally Responsive Facilitative Practices

It is a brisk fall day, the first week of October, and I am huddled with students at a round table in the school library. It's lunchtime, and I've brought snacks for everyone, a variety of chip bags from our bodega across the street and some fruit for Karla, who insists, "We gotta eat healthier, people!" This is our first meeting together, and it is a co-ed group of five 10th-graders. We begin by sharing our preferred names and identifiers. I start, "You can call me Jody. I identify as white, cisgender, female."

The students follow my lead, with Danny sharing that he identifies as "gay and Filipino," Karla as a "bisexual Latinx female," Clifford as a "straight Black male," Justine as "a Puerto Rican bisexual female," and Julia as an "undecided, cisgender Spanish female."

I then talk to the group about why I created these book clubs and ask them to share why they have joined. The conversation takes a lively turn, with students talking about their favorite books. Danny grabs one of the texts resting on our table, declaring, "This one looks good! What's this about?"

Responding to his interest, I decide to ignore my planned agenda, and we dive right into the books, discussing what we want to read and why. The group eventually settles on *Upstate* (Buckhanon, 2006).

"I think now we should set up some norms, or ground rules, for our conversations, so that we can create a space that feels comfortable and safe," I explain.

"Stay on task!" Karla shouts immediately.

"Can I write?" begs Danny, grabbing the chart paper and markers from under the table.

"Of course!" I smile. "Go for it. Karla, what do you mean by 'stay on task'?"

"Don't stray away from the conversation."

"Okay," I say. "What if the book relates to something in our lives and we want to talk about it, especially if it connects to the book?"

"Yeah, that makes sense," Karla responds. "But what I'm saying is that let's not get to the point where we're talking about stuff that happened in school that has nothing to do with the books. That's like if we're talking about that chair and then someone just brings up what happened last Monday in the lunchroom. What does that have to do with the chair? Nothing."

"Got it," I reassure Karla. "How about maybe 'stay on topic'? Would that work?"

"Yup! There you go!" Karla confirms and the other students nod in agreement, as Danny writes the first norm on our chart paper.

"Clifford, what do you think?" I ask.

"Be respectful of other people's emotions and feelings," he offers. "Really be respectful. You know, keep it cool."

"Keep it cool?" I repeat. "I like that. Be respectful; keep it cool. Julia, what do you think?"

"I don't know," she says softly, tilting her head to the ground. "Maybe be sure that everyone has a voice?"

"That's terrific!" I praise her.

"Also, participate!" shouts Danny, as he continues writing with great precision on our shared chart paper.

"No interrupting too," says Karla. "I hate that. I'm trying to talk and people sometimes talk over me. I don't like that."

"How do you spell that? Interrupt?" Danny asks.

"Sound it out, Danny!" Karla jokes.

"I have trouble with that word too," I say. "Let's do it together."

We work out the spelling collectively, and I suggest, in jest, "You can also just write it real sloppy so that no one will know we don't know how to spell it."

Danny rolls his eyes and exclaims, "Never." He reaches for his phone for accuracy.

"Danny, it's your turn!" Karla yells. The librarian shoots a disapproving look at us, and I signal with my hand for the group to keep their voices down.

"What do you think, man?" Danny whispers to Clifford.

"I think it's best that you come up with the next rule right now," Clifford quips.

"Do your homework," suggests Danny, shrugging his shoulders.

"Wait, this isn't class," I remind them. "Do we have homework here?"

"Okay, how about do your reading?" Danny revises.

"Sounds great," I reply. "Let's get that up there."

"Wait, one more," says Justine. "We should be open-minded."

"Be open-minded," says Danny. "That's good."

"Clifford, what's up?" Karla asks. "You seem to be taking in a lot of what we're saying."

"I'm a sponge," he explains. "I'm absorbing."

"I think it's okay for us to go in and out of this space," I say. "You know, talk when we want, absorb when we want. There are no pressures. This is a terrific start on the agreements, and we can add to them as we go along. We're almost out of time, though; the bell is gonna ring soon. Let's debrief at the end of each meeting, so we can talk about our process and how things are going. Can you share what worked and what didn't work so that we can improve as we go along? What did you think?"

"Better than expected," Danny begins. "I really thought that we were gonna come over here and just read. Nothing else, no discussing. There's nothing wrong with reading, but I'm glad that we spoke too."

"Yeah, I'm really excited to read this book," added Karla. "I like that we get to choose them and we can come and talk about what we thought."

"I like that we have these rules too," Justine said. "You know, if things get crazy and out of control."

The group laughs and begins joking about "book clubs gone wild." Clifford raises his hand patiently. Danny asks, "Why are you raising your hand?"

"That's the last rule, man. Let's have fun."

"I think that's a great rule, Clifford," I smile. "Let's commit to that."

This anecdote captures one way in which we, as facilitators, can ensure that our spaces are student-centered, culturally sustaining, and inclusive.

- **Student-Centered:** Students drive the agenda and conversations.
- **Culturally Sustaining:** Students select books that connect to their shared interests and lived experiences.
- **Inclusive:** Students set agreements so that their voices are heard and valued.

In this chapter, we're going to begin with how we can create student-centered school communities and classrooms that provide rich grounds for pedagogical practices such as book clubs. I will then discuss some of the dispositions and approaches needed for facilitation, specifically speaking to the ways we can use culturally sustaining and emotionally responsive approaches with our students, practices that are trauma-informed and healing-centered. We will also dive into how we can structure our first book club sessions so that we create environments that feel safe for students and allow them to be courageous and supportive to one another.

WHAT DOES IT MEAN TO BE A CULTURALLY SUSTAINING AND EMOTIONALLY RESPONSIVE FACILITATOR?

In our first chapter, I asked you to reflect on your own identities, communities, and literacies as adolescents and adults. In Chapter 2, I asked you to reflect on your students and their identities, abilities, languages, and literacies.

Self-reflection is the first step to becoming an effective facilitator; we need to continually think about ourselves and our experiences and how those may overlap or diverge from those of our students. Who we are impacts how we engage with youth. In this section, I will return to this point and provide actions and dispositions that will help us to work to become more culturally sustaining and healing-centered facilitators.

#1: Reflect on your identities and lived experiences and be transparent about them with your students. During the pandemic when schools were remote, the school counselor and I collaborated to create book clubs for youth while we were under quarantine. During that time, George Floyd was murdered. As white women, working with young immigrant men of color, three from Africa and three from Bangladesh, we knew our role as facilitators was precarious. Before that book club meeting, the counselor and I met to name the experience and our privilege, thus developing ways to engage in conversations with care and compassion. We did not ignore the event, and we did not forget our own privilege or complicity in systemic racism and police brutality. And so I began the book club as follows:

"We want to acknowledge what happened with George Floyd and the outrage that has followed. While we are white women who benefit from our racial position, we do not condone nor support brutality against Black and Brown men and women. We want to give you this space, if you need it, to put our book aside, and see if there are any issues or feelings you want to share. You may not feel comfortable doing so with us, and if that is the case, we have others at our school, adult men of color, who we can connect you with, who you may need to process some of those emotions. But we do want to give you that opportunity now, if you need it."

For the rest of that session, the school counselor and I ignored the book and we sat silently. Listening and learning. We also had support systems in place in case students needed other outlets (i.e., male counselors of color who meet with students in affinity groups). And while we could never imagine the pain and fear these young men experience because of our own privilege and positionality, we did feel it necessary to provide the space to discuss what happened. We were transparent about our privilege and positions of power, and we were transparent about the discomfort of having that conversation with our students. We named it, owned it, and assured them that we too wanted to disrupt the system that continues to murder Black and Brown men and women.

In working within diverse communities, our identities and lived experiences will inevitably be different from those of our students. Nieto (2010) urges adults who work with youth to examine their identities and positionalities. We must consider our students' intersectionalities, as well as our own. As a Latinx male teacher, how are you engaging with Muslim women in your classroom? As a heterosexual female, how are you engaging with transgender students? As facilitators, we must understand our students' plurality of identities and use them as assets for the foundation of our book clubs. This work of getting to know ourselves and our students must be ongoing, as must be our commitment to marginalized and vulnerable youth.

#2: Get to know your students. In addition to self-reflection, we must get to know our students. This can be done informally, speaking to them before or after book clubs in the hallways or between classes. It also may mean allowing time before, during, and after book clubs for students to share pieces of themselves—about their identities and communities.

Think back to those life maps from Chapter 2; that is one creative way to get to know your students. An alternative to the maps is identity wheels, another way we can graphically display our intersectional identities (see the website for a sample). On the "spokes" of the wheel, students can share their cultural and linguistic identities along with their ability diversities. In the center of the wheel, they can offer other markers of who they are, such as sister, daughter, artist, or reader. If students feel comfortable sharing, any of these creative endeavors can be displayed in the classroom or the book club space. In the past, I have also had students write their "auto-literacy-biographies." In these pieces, students share information about their identities, communities, and literacies. I also write my own auto-literacy-biography so that they can get to know me. Students can also choose to write in their preferred genre as well, a narrative, spoken word piece, or creative video instead. The idea is to offer students choice in how they want to represent themselves.

Another way to get to know students and their literacy backgrounds is through conferences. On the website is a protocol for these, which generally take about 10–15 minutes, depending on your style of engagement and the student. The protocol includes first asking students about themselves and their literacies. Students then select a text of their choice (either informational or narrative) to read aloud to me. During this time, I can listen and assess their decoding and fluency skills. Afterward, I ask follow-up questions to assess their comprehension and learn more about them as readers. If facilitating book clubs outside of the classroom, I recommend holding these conferences before meeting as a whole group. If you are a classroom teacher, I recommend doing these sessions the first weeks of school. For me, I conducted the conferences during independent reading and writing time. If you have 25 students, for example, and can do the conferences twice per period every day, then the work may take the whole month. Though time intensive to be sure, conducting these conferences has been the most powerful method I have used to get to know my students and build relationships with them.

#3: Listen. Pause. Listen some more. Facilitators must be strong listeners. We need to hear our students' stories, perspectives, and connections with texts and to one another. Simultaneously, we must pause often. Allow students to be the voices most heard in book club. When you find yourself ready to say something or ask a question: Pause. Wait. Listen.

Remember that these book clubs are not about you. They are about our students. These are their spaces, and if we want them to be truly student-centered, we must let students lead the conversations, generate the questions, and connect.

We also should listen to our students' body language. Has someone put their head down? Has someone turned their body away from the group? Is someone leaving to go to the bathroom and not returning? Listen to their bodies—and check in. Is everything okay? When students respond in ways that seem disengaged or if discomfort seems apparent, we need to find out what is going on, preferably in private spaces—and not in public in front of others.

#4: Use trauma-informed and healing-centered approaches. As facilitators, we must remember not to make assumptions. Ever. We can work to eliminate confusion and conflict if we just ask questions, especially trauma-informed and healing-centered questions. As an example, one year while facilitating book clubs in the classroom, I noticed that William put his head down on his desk. I walked up to him, kneeled so that we were eye to eye, and asked, "Is everything okay? Wanna take a break?"

William nodded as tears filled his eyes. He grabbed the bathroom pass, and when I saw him slip outside of the room, I asked my co-teacher if she could handle the class on her own. She agreed, and I stepped out to talk with William, who revealed his parents were divorcing. As trauma-informed and healing-centered facilitators, we must get to the root of the problems—instead of creating more. We can do this by asking questions that are emotionally responsive to the moment.

Minahan (2019) offers other strategies facilitators can use to be more trauma-informed, suggesting that we

- **expect** unexpected responses and put our students' reactions to curriculum, us, and their peers in context of what may be going on in their lived experiences;
- **employ** thoughtful actions with students and build relationships with them. An example of this is to always be transparent about our instructional choices, such as, Why are we doing book clubs? Why are we reading these books?
- **promote** predictability and consistency, which for the context of this book means meeting regularly and offering consistent routines that are clear to students. Predictable routines provide students with a sense of safety;
- **provide** students with an out. If things are not working on a particular day in book club, have an alternative that is engaging and healing-centered that students can participate in so that they feel safe and

successful. I had a corner of my room where students could grab paper, markers, and sticky notes to journal or do artwork about their feelings.

Much of the work done by a facilitator involves being trauma-informed, which means committing to the social-emotional learning of our students but also to social justice and anti-oppression. Researchers and practitioners in trauma-informed approaches (Love, 2019; Simmons, 2020a, 2020b) ask that we be more aware and intentional about how we address the adverse effects of racialized violence that our students witness and experience. Simmons (2020b), for example, urges us to imagine the impact of being erased from academic content while also being visible to "over-surveillance, policing, and demoralizing media coverage" and how that impacts Black and Brown students. Further, Simmons asks, "What do white children learn from these very same triggering images of Black death and the white-centered curricula?" (p. 80). Ultimately, they can replicate the damage and thus learn how to erase and dehumanize the lives of their Black and Brown peers. Our work around trauma, then, must not only address the stresses of racism but also give space for white students to confront their privilege. Simmons explains, "Racial trauma work is just as necessary for white children because the ignorance and bias that feeds racism, which originates from the acceptance of white supremacy, inflict harm, too" (p. 80).

The same ideologies apply to other historically and currently marginalized students: for our Asian and Asian American students who must endure the model minority myth narratives; for our students who identify as LGBTQ and experience bullying and stereotyping; for our undocumented and immigrant students who receive continual messaging of not belonging; for our students with disabilities who experience low teacher expectations and separate spaces. We must acknowledge the roles that these identities play in our students' mental health, in the ways they experience anxiety and depression and the ways in which they must manage the systemic and everyday acts of discrimination and oppression (McGee & Stovall, 2015).

In short, we cannot *do* the work of trauma-informed instruction without understanding and incorporating our knowledge of systemic oppressions into the ways we engage with students (Gorski, 2020). Thus, "the best trauma-informed practices are rooted in anti-racism, and anti-oppression more broadly" (Gorski, 2020, p. 17). While unpacking narratives of trauma in our texts may feel uncomfortable, leaving out these histories is irresponsible and silences the diverse experiences of our students. Jones (2020) advises, "We must *want* to do the right thing by our students, even if that means we have to struggle to learn more and seek feedback from students about the impact of our curricular choices" (p. 50). This translates into asking our students to be co-curricular designers, digging into what is working and not working and how we can refine instruction to be more responsive to their emotions, needs, and interests.

Further, Ginwright (2018) calls on practitioners to peel back the layers of trauma-informed pedagogies, explaining that we should take more healing-centered approaches with students. This means being inclusive of culture, civic action, and healing, viewing trauma as not just isolated, individual events but as shared experiences that can be overcome and disrupted through collective action and healing. Baker-Bell, Jones Stanbrough, and Everett (2017) offer similar advice, explaining we can view pedagogies of healing in using two tools:

- "tools to heal," which acknowledge wounds exist and then identify the culprit, and
- "tools to transform," which respond to the wound and work to transform the conditions that caused it. (p. 139)

When we select and discuss books with our students, we cannot ignore the oppressions our students experience. Thus, we must be vigilant not to retraumatize them through our textual selections and questioning, but instead provide space for conversations that allow students freedom and safety to speak to their issues and concerns and simultaneously give them space to help build one another up. In Chapter 6, we will focus on using book clubs as forums to identify and analyze bias and oppression and to use those conversations for advocacy.

For now, as facilitators, we must commit to creating safe spaces such as book clubs, where we can center the healing processes that students need and that may arise out of the content of our books and the lived experiences of our students.

#5: Acknowledge, support, and praise students for their participation and involvement in the conversations. In my experience, students often select books that connect to their lives. For example, you might have a group of students who identify as transgender or genderfluid and thus read books such as *Felix Ever After* (Callender, 2020) or *I Am J* (Beam, 2012). Both of these texts provide perspectives of youth of color who are dealing with their sexual and gender identities. In reading such texts, students may engage in conversations that become charged or painful. As facilitators, we can acknowledge that pain and then ask them questions so that they can opt out or dig deeper, especially when our texts deal with such sensitive issues as coming out or transitioning.

Once during a book club session, a student shared that she had been sexually assaulted. The first thing I told her was "Thank you for sharing such a difficult experience. That takes courage. As a survivor of sexual assault, I understand how hard it can be to talk about this kind of trauma. Do you want to say more on that, or should we let it lie as it is?"

Felicia chose to let it lie, and afterward, I referred her to our social worker to get the kind of support I could not provide. In this situation, and in all cases like it, we want to acknowledge our students' feelings and praise them immediately for their courage, and we want to do so often, especially when students share their connections to texts and how they intersect with their lives. This allows students to feel validated and supported in what they've shared. Simultaneously, in this particular instance, I also wanted Felicia to know that I could take risks and share my own experiences with trauma. At the time, I did not have to dig deep into our shared experience. And I certainly did not want to unsettle or trigger more trauma—nor did I want to force Felicia to share more details. My ultimate goal was to provide an inclusive, safe, and brave space where she and her peers could feel comfortable sharing their thoughts and feelings. Our role is to support students, to praise and validate, and then to provide them with additional services they may need.

At the same time, we must monitor *our monitoring* of students' feelings. What does that mean? Sometimes the books that we read and our conversations may cause students to experience a range of emotions: from joy and anger to frustration and sadness. We must be vigilant in not suppressing these emotions as they arise. Anger, for example, may be an emotion that causes us discomfort, but to suppress our students' anger or frustration is to say that their outrage is not valid (Kaler-Jones, 2020). That anger and frustration can become a powerful way to channel our students' quest for justice. So, monitor your own emotions as you listen and learn from your students. And remember the constant fallback: Listen, pause, listen more, and praise.

#6: Be prepared and flexible. These actions may seem contradictory but they are essential. Sometimes our book clubs will be quiet, and it's going to be awkward, so we need to be prepared for ways to step in so that we can get students engaged with one another. In the next chapter, I will provide sample agendas that we can use to ensure that the book club conversations are fluid, inclusive, and student-centered.

At the same time, we need to be okay with dumping agendas. It's always good to be prepared, but we also have to let students lead. The idea is that these book clubs eventually run themselves without you. The ultimate goal is that students don't need us anymore. We want them to be independent and collaborative without our direction. And when they don't need you, your job has been accomplished.

#7: Monitor and revise as necessary. Think back to that opening anecdote in this chapter where I asked students to reflect on the process of book club at the end of the meeting. Having students self-reflect and debrief the conversations is critical so that they can improve as they go along. Simultaneously, we must be diligent about taking note of our students' progress and then revising our processes to meet their needs.

For example, I had one book club of all middle school boys who continually taunted one another, calling each other names and teasing one another. For our next meeting, I started with a lesson called "Let's be kind to each other." We talked about what it means to be kind—what it looked and sounded like. And then we talked about why it was important within our book club. This is not to say the young men changed through that one mini-lesson and discussion—but it was something we needed to improve. Being explicit about what we expect is important. Equally critical is helping students get there. And eventually we did. Yes, the young men continued to taunt and tease one another probably outside of class but in our one hour per week, book club became a space where we learned to be kinder to one another.

#8: Collaborate with your peers. When I started doing book clubs outside of the classroom, where the priority was to focus on culturally affirming social-emotional learning, I connected with our social worker, Danilo. Once a week, I spoke to him about the kinds of conversations we had in book clubs, and he let me observe him while he met with students (only if students agreed, of course).

I learned so much from that experience, specifically how to engage in trauma-informed and healing-centered approaches. How to handle charged situations. How to be more patient. How to listen. Years later, when at another school, I collaborated with another counselor to facilitate book clubs.

The point here is that we need to work with others when providing youth book club spaces. As educators, administrators, and support staff, we have much to learn from our counseling folks, who can help us be more emotionally responsive to students. As administrators, counselors, and staff, we have much to learn from our teachers about engaging with literacies. We must learn from and turn to each other, as then we become stronger and more capable of offering richer, holistic practices for our students.

#9: Bring joy. Book clubs can be heavy, and we can use these spaces for the important work of self-reflection, storytelling, and critical connection and analysis. We can also use these spaces to help lift each other up and imagine ways to create actions for justice and equity. In doing this work, we must also bring joy, humor, laughter, and lightness. Remember Clifford's words: "That's the last rule . . . let's have fun." Doing heavy work requires that we take care of each other—as taking care of ourselves is ultimately an act of justice. So, bring joy to your spaces and give yourself and your students access to what makes us wholly human.

WHAT HAPPENS DURING OUR FIRST BOOK CLUB SESSION?

Now that we've established some groundings for book club facilitation, let's discuss that first meeting. This list offers suggested materials to bring:

- ☐ **Your agenda** (See below for a sample.)
- ☐ **Copies of the books:** Try to have at least one book for each student in your space. If you have five students, then bring at least five books.

If you have 20 students, then you need 20 books. These should be books that you have multiple copies of. For example, suppose I am a teacher and beginning book clubs that center the lives of Muslim youth and address Islamophobia. In that case, I might have five copies of each of the following: *Saints and Misfits* (Ali, 2018), *Internment* (Ahmed, 2020), *Love, Hate and Other Filters* (Ahmed, 2019), and *The Love and Lies of Rukhsana Ali* (Khan, 2019). If I am doing an out-of-classroom book club—or I have a very small class of five—then I would only have one copy of each text. The goal is to provide students with choice and ensure that each student has one book in hand as we decide what we will read.

☐ **Copies of book pass guides:** A book pass guide is a graphic organizer where students record their interactions with the texts they can choose from. For example, they might look at five different books, studying each for about 5 minutes, looking at the front cover and reading the back and first few pages. During this time, on the book pass guide, they write down the title, the author, their rating (on a scale from 1 to 5), and their opinions of the text. Once they've reviewed the book, they pass the text to another student and receive a new one to evaluate. (See the website for a sample guide.)

☐ **Materials for students to engage with the texts:** These materials depend on the ways in which you and the students will actively read the texts. This could include role sheets (which we will talk about in the next chapter), journals, sticky notes, or graphic organizers. The idea is that students are engaging with the texts actively as they read. We want them to, for example, ask questions and make connections, so we need to have a protocol in place for what that will look like. Perhaps it will be different for every student. Perhaps one student uses sticky notes, one uses a graphic organizer, and another uses a journal. Again, we want to provide choice, not just in *what* they read but in *how* they engage with the content.

Whether doing book clubs outside or inside the classroom, we should always plan and prepare agendas. This will help you and your students use the limited time you have. The sample agenda provided here is not meant to be prescriptive—just some suggestions for organizing the time. For me, the process takes about two days, but for others, it could take shorter or longer. It really depends on the context of your setting and your students.

DAY ONE

1. **Introductions:** For classroom teachers who have already integrated those community-building events into their classroom, this will not be necessary. However, if you are meeting with your book club for

the first time, you'll want to make sure that everyone introduces themselves—including you! You might ask:

 » What is your preferred name and gender identity?
 » What brings you to book club? What do you hope to get out of this experience?
 » What's the best book you've ever read?

These sample introductory questions should be differentiated based on your students and the purpose of your book club. For example, if you organize an out-of-classroom book club about LGBTQ issues, the questions might be, Why are you here today? What do you hope to get out of book clubs? What do you want to learn about LGBTQ issues?

2. **Book Club Purpose and Process Discussion:** This portion of the agenda discusses what book clubs are. Why are we doing these? What purpose do they serve? It's important to be clear about the reasons you are creating these spaces. I like to open these discussions with conversations around humanizing dialogue—and what that looks and sounds like (Nouri & Sajjadi, 2014). Thus, I introduce to students some elements for safe and inclusive book clubs:

 » Critical thinking, reading, and discussions about the text and the world
 » Mutual and reciprocal trust
 » Love for both the world and for others
 » Humility, the belief that we all are learning from each other
 » Faith and hope in the process, in the connections to each other, and in justice (Nouri & Sajjadi, 2014)

I then ask students if they would like to add to this list. What are the elements that you want to see as we work together?

Once we've shared our purposes for book clubs, we talk about our agreements, which we saw in the opening anecdote of this chapter. It's critical that our students collaboratively develop these so that youth have ownership over the process. I suggest putting those co-constructed norms on chart paper so that you and your students can revise them—and so that there is a constant reminder of the shared expectations. A final suggestion is to phrase your agreements in positive language instead of deficit-framed discourse. For example, replace "don't be mean" with "be kind to each other" or replace "don't interrupt" with "listen actively."

3. **Book Club Scenario Activity:** I provide students with a list of scenarios that could happen during book club to be prepared for when they occur. I usually put one scenario each on a slip of paper and pass them out to students. If in a small group, each student can read their scenario aloud and then we can discuss. If in a larger class, students can partner up or meet in small groups to share how they

would address these scenarios. We then discuss these situations as a whole group while I take notes for students for future reference. Scenarios could include the following:

» What if I am absent from book club?
» What if I don't like the book?
» What if I don't do the reading?
» What if I finish the book before others?
» What if I get upset or sad as I read?
» What if someone in the group gets angry or sad during our book club?

4. **Book Pass:** This next part of the agenda is where we get to play with the books. When in a small group, I have a stack of books in front of us to peruse. If I'm in a larger class, students sit in small groups with a stack of different books at their tables. (Think back to Shahnaj and her book tasting experience from Chapter 2.) The next step is to provide students with a book pass guide and model how to fill it out.

» Where do I find the title and author?
» How can I preview the book? By looking at the cover, by reading the back and the first page. I tell students reading that first page is important to get a sense of the book's reading level. Are there more than five words that I don't know on that first page? If so, it might be too hard. Do I like the author's writing style? Is the font size too big or too small?
» Students then provide a number of 1 (the lowest) to 5 (the highest) of their level of interest in the book.
» After they've considered all the choices, they tell me what their top two books are at the bottom of their sheet. If I am in a large classroom, I collect these and the next day I finish the rest of the agenda, starting with letting students know which book club they will be in. If I'm with a smaller book club, outside of class, then we share our scores for each text and collectively negotiate what we will all read together. We usually decide our book right on the spot, and depending on time, finish the agenda below or wait until our next meeting.

DAY TWO

5. **Distribution of Materials:** The next step is to provide students with materials, based on the type of book clubs you've decided to facilitate. As I explained briefly above—and as will be explained in more depth in our next chapter—you have several options for materials based on the needs of your students. Therefore, you might provide role sheets, sticky notes, graphic organizers, or journals.

6. **Shared Reading:** Some of you may decide that your book clubs will meet every day and students will read together every day. Some of you will only hold book clubs once, twice, or three times a week. Regardless of your decision, it is critical to read that first chapter or section of the text together. (A solid 15–30 minutes of reading allows for a rich conversation.) The purpose of shared reading is to build community and generate interest and motivation, especially for students who may be reluctant to read. Perhaps you have a strong reader read the chapter aloud or provide an audio version for students to listen to as they read. Even better, you read the book aloud. Students who are emergent readers need your fluent voice to help guide them through the words. Sometimes, I'll read the narrative aloud and then have students read the dialogue to bring the text to life with multiple voices. Again, the choice is up to you, but be sure that you have that opening shared experience with your students.

7. **Discussion:** That first book club discussion can be tricky. In some instances, I've had students bursting to talk after we read. In some cases, it has been radio silence and crickets. Be prepared and flexible for either. With some students, I find asking them to write before we discuss useful to collect their thoughts before sharing with others. Regardless of what you decide, these are some more generalized questions you can ask after the reading is done:
   - » What are your initial thoughts on the book?
   - » What do you think of the writing style?
   - » Did you make any connections with the text as you read?
   - » What kinds of questions came up for you as you read?

   In a large classroom, you can provide these questions to your youth-led book clubs. Students can choose which questions to respond to in writing and then share aloud as a group. When I am facilitating a small group, I always annotate my copy of the text (i.e., highlight sections of the book or place sticky notes with questions on them) so that I'm prepared with additional questions in case we have time and students are a bit reticent. With my school counselor, when we co-led book clubs remotely during the pandemic, we always met the morning before book clubs to discuss our priority topics in case students were quiet, hesitant, or shy.

8. **Planning Our Reading:** In smaller book clubs with you and the students, now is the time to plan the reading ahead. How much will we read by next week? If your book clubs are for a fixed time and you are a classroom teacher, you'll need more long-term planning. If, for example, book clubs are a 6-week unit, then have students divide up the book by 6, so they know how many pages to read each week. On the website is a handout that students can fill out as a group so that they hold each other accountable for the reading. During this

time, groups also set goals for themselves—things they want to commit
to each other. In the past, my students have shared such goals as: *We
promise to finish our reading by Fridays. We promise to be kind to
each other and make sure that everyone has a voice. We promise to
support one another if someone is struggling or needs help.*

9. **Closing Reflections:** This is an opportunity for students to share how
they're feeling. You might ask: What is one thing you learned from
someone? What is one thing you realized you had in common with
someone? You might ask what they are excited about for future book
clubs—or what they are nervous about. You might ask them to make
a prediction about the book: What do they think will happen next?
You might even ask when and where they will do their reading for
book club. This helps students to visualize and commit to locations
and times for their reading. If it's a Friday afternoon, you might
just ask them their plans for the weekend. The idea is to use these
last 5 minutes to reflect on the process and the book, while also
continuing to build community.

Now that we've established some foundations for book clubs, let's pause and
think about our next steps. What actions can you take now—and what planning can you begin? In our next chapter, we will dive into how to sustain and
maintain our book clubs.

Building Community and Capacity
What will be the agenda for the first book club meeting?
What materials will you need?
What will be the introductory activities and questions to build safety and community?

APPLYING WIDER LENSES:
BOOK CLUBS AND OUR LARGER SCHOOL CONTEXTS

Before moving forward to more book club practicalities, I want us to consider book clubs from a wider lens, particularly how they fit within our larger
school communities. Many of us may be in schools where we work collectively, where teachers, families, administrators, and staff work to enact

systems for equity. However, many of us may not work in this kind of environment. I will offer suggestions for you to think more broadly about your schools. Read through these—and think about what might work for you and your school, and if they feel too overwhelming, then know that book clubs alone can be a compelling way to transform the lives of young people.

My first recommendation when exploring systemic change at the school level is conducting an equity audit (Capper & Young, 2015; Green, 2017; Skrla, McKenzie, & Scheurich, 2009). The ultimate goal of an audit is to unearth and disrupt institutional practices that produce and sustain oppressive and discriminatory systems. Audits are a process for applying a magnifying glass to how our communities talk about and engage with students, particularly for those who are most vulnerable and marginalized. Skrla et al. (2009) recommend teachers, administrators, and school personnel look at three different areas:

1. **Programmatic Equity:** Which populations of students are underrepresented in honors and AP classes and which ones are overrepresented in special education and skills-based courses? Which groups are disciplined more often than others? How are we maintaining relationships with our surrounding community and with our students' families? How are we serving students holistically? Are we paying equal attention to students' social-emotional needs as these intersect with their academics? Are we coming from asset- and justice-oriented perspectives?
2. **Quality of Teaching and Support-Based Services:** Are our teachers, administrators, and support staff representative of our students? Which educators are teaching students with the greatest needs, and why? How are teachers using culturally sustaining and culturally affirming trauma-informed instruction? How are we providing mental health services that are culturally and trauma-informed?
3. **Achievement Equity:** What are the opportunity and access gaps? How are we measuring student progress, including and beyond standardized tests? What do our attendance, retention, and graduation rates look like? How are we connecting to families, and what is their role in our school?

The process of conducting an equity audit involves several steps, including bringing multiple people together. This can be suggested to your administration—or if you are an administrator, this is something that you can begin in collaboration with school personnel.

This brings me to my **second recommendation**, which is creating an equity team that could plan the audit. Many of your schools may already have a team, so you can recommend that they conduct an audit. If you don't have an equity team, perhaps this is something you want to recommend to administration. Keep in mind that this team should include diverse perspectives, identities, and positionalities, including teachers, students, families, support staff, and administration. All meetings should occur on a routine and consistent basis.

Whether you create an equity team or develop an audit, there are other activities you can introduce to your school as a way to collect data on equity-based practices. Perhaps a school team reviews school and discipline policies that reinforce white supremacy (e.g., policing what students are wearing, maintaining no-tolerance rules) or looks at the school's website to see how accessible it is to diverse families. Is information easy to locate and offered in multiple languages? The administration might also decide to distribute surveys or conduct interviews and focus groups with families, students, support staff, and faculty. At one of my previous schools, we had a local, trusted community member interview and record students about their schooling experiences; we then shared these videos with faculty and staff during a professional development day. Our students' voices were pivotal in moving people to see how our practices were not culturally informed nor sustaining. Students spoke to what it was like to only see white teachers and to see curriculum that reflected primarily white narratives. It was a powerful experience that centered student voice and allowed our administration, staff, and teachers to begin reflecting on and transforming their work.

Other activities can be more informal. Consider shadowing students, where teachers, administration, and staff get an eye-opening experience of what a day looks like for students. If the administration is able to organize these events, I recommend following different student populations: students with disabilities, students who identify as LGBTQ, emergent bi- and multilingual students, students from a variety of ethnicities and religious identities. The goal is to observe schooling from the perspectives and lived experiences of our students. What are they learning? How are they engaging with their peers? When are they eating? Do they have enough time to get to class and use the bathroom? Once faculty, staff, and administration shadow students, administration can lead conversations with the school community about reform so that our practices and services are more student-informed and equity-based.

Another activity is called a "piece of the pie," where students from a variety of identities, backgrounds, and ability levels collect all the "paper" they receive in their classes. This can be done throughout a week or a month. The equity team then assesses the kinds of written materials students are engaging with. Are the materials culturally representative? Do they have a justice-based lens? Are they student-centered and differentiated? This kind of assessment allows us to reconsider professional learning, where administration can use the data to drive the content for professional development days.

Walk-throughs are another activity to consider. In teams, school personnel utilize a checklist of the types of evidence for equity-based pedagogical practices (see the website for a sample). In the past, I have led this activity as a literacy coach, asking individuals in diverse roles in the school, including teachers, staff, and administration, to observe hallways, classrooms, and shared spaces. We looked for the ways our students' identities were represented in our spaces. Did we see student work in the hallways and classrooms? Were the pieces of art, posters, bulletin boards reflective of our students' diversities? In our classrooms, did we see the same? Did we see culturally relevant texts or word walls? Did we see students reading and writing independently and teachers providing scaffolds? Was there a focus on advocacy and social justice? We then used these walk-throughs as a way to transform our environment. In fact, on one professional development day, we spent the entire morning revamping our spaces based on what we observed and learned from the walk-through process.

Data gathering takes time—and should never stop as we want to continually assess how we are doing with our students and how we are connecting with their families. Once data are collected, it's important to have schoolwide conversations to discuss the findings and then develop and implement solutions. How can we address the gaps that the data demonstrate? Further, how will we monitor the solutions that we put in place?

Another way schools can use data is through transformation of school spaces. After doing walk-throughs, we might ask ourselves: How can we create spaces that represent and celebrate our students and their histories, literacies, and communities? Further, how can we create spaces that are literacy-rich and engage students in models for social justice?

For readers who may not be able to do this work collectively in their schools, perhaps consider just changing the landscapes of your particular areas within your school. We want our hallways, for example, to be filled with student work, from youth solving math problems to engaging in creative projects. We want bulletin boards that honor diverse leaders, historians, artists, and writers. Love (2019) reminds us that we cannot provide liberation for students without celebrating their joy, particularly for Black and Brown youth, who have been marginalized within our curricula, whose only narratives are told through lenses of trauma. So bring joy to your spaces, and simultaneously, use your imagination to build critical consciousness. For instance, your hallway bulletin boards can provide information about community events that occur near your schools and ways students can engage in advocacy. In my previous high school, long before we had an equity team, we created a social justice club and marched together for #BlackLivesMatter. Many of our faculty and staff also collaborated with students to rally against gentrification efforts in our school's neighborhood.

Shared spaces in your schools can be also be great places to promote literacies. Consider keeping bookshelves with young adult literature in the front office and counselors' offices. While students wait, they can peruse books and find engaging texts that reflect their experiences. (These areas are also an effective spot to place your recruitment flyers!) In the past, as a coach, I asked staff, administration, and teachers to display posters on their doors that highlighted what they were reading by providing a book synopsis. We want to model to students that we read, too. If you are a teacher and feel that you may not have influence on the larger systems or spaces in your school communities, then focus on your classrooms, as these locations are critically important. How do we arrange desks? Are they in rows that might discourage dialogue and collaboration, or are they arranged in small groups or pairs? Are our classrooms filled with diverse texts? Is student work displayed? Do we have images of diverse leaders in our disciplines hanging on our walls?

The central crux of my argument here is that book clubs are critical—*and* they are part of the larger context within our schools. Therefore, we want to transform our environments and systems so they are inclusive and working toward justice. All of you have a different kind of influence in your school community—so think through these recommendations and consider what will work best for you. Perhaps it is transforming your classroom or your office or the hallways that surround your space. Perhaps you are an administrator and you try out some of the larger recommendations above, or perhaps you are a teacher or counselor who offers some recommendations to your administration. These are meant to be a spectrum of ideas, some of which will work in your context and some of which may not.

Regardless, think through how you can create spaces that center students' identities, their cultural and linguistic pluralism, and their accomplishments. In collectively developing landscapes that highlight diverse voices, languages, and perspectives, we are one step closer to ensuring our environments are inclusive. Further, we want to build our communities' critical consciousness, letting our walls breathe justice, speak multiple languages, and celebrate diverse literacies. This is the kind of space we can imagine and build; this is also the kind of space where we can create rich, nurturing contexts for book clubs.

QR Code for Chapter 3 Resources

CHAPTER 4

Maintaining, Sustaining, and Assessing Book Club Conversations

Today I'm working with an in-class book club in a school specifically for neurodiverse students. The group consists of five adolescents who all identify as white and have been diagnosed with autism. They have chosen to read *Atypical: Life With Asperger's in 20⅓ Chapters* (Saperstein, 2010), a memoir of short essays written by a young man who has Asperger's Syndrome. Nelson, Steven, Mike, Sarah, and Richard have a close rapport with one another. While Sarah is the only female in the group, she refuses to be silenced by the others, who sometimes dominate our conversations. Mike is the quietest and the one member of book club who has yet to speak in the 3 months we have worked together. He keeps up with the reading, though, and when we meet, he usually walks about the room, listening in. I often hear him snicker at Nelson's and Steven's jokes or shout abruptly when he enjoys a passage we are reading. We meet once a week, and each week, Mike gets closer and closer to our circle, sometimes standing, sometimes sitting. Today his chair is just outside our group, and Sarah has moved her position so she is not blocking his view. It is the closest he has interacted with us since we began.

We start our session with check-ins about our personal lives. Once everyone has shared, I ask students to summarize what we have read for today, which Steven does with enthusiastic detail. Sarah interjects here and there to add in plot points that Steven has overlooked. I then ask students to share passages they connected to, passages that resonated with their lives. Steven shares first, then Sarah and Nelson. I too read a quote I appreciated:

> *I am also quasi-prepared for the consequences of imposing myself on people who choose to condemn AS as a character flaw in need of correction rather than compassion. . . . It is not enough for me and other AS individuals to settle for "tolerance." Tolerance is just an unstable compromise between the neurotypical public and those individuals judged as . . . atypical . . . someday the DSM-IV will hopefully be revised to include the common traits of integrity and perseverance. (pp. 137–140)*

After the reading, I ask, "What do you think? It's a tough quote to unpack."

Steven responds, "It's a lot easier to understand if you *actually* have Asperger's—"

Sarah rolls her eyes, interjecting, "I think he's saying he's gonna keep on raising awareness and trying to have people be nicer."

"And not always look at the negative," Steven adds.

Sarah continues, "Autism is not an illness or shouldn't be seen as one because that's really hurtful. You've got to see it as normal."

"It's actually seen as a disorder and not a sickness," Richard clarifies.

"That's what I mean, though," Sarah agrees. "Let me live my life. They're always talking about wanting to cure autism but most people that have autism don't care for a cure. They just want love."

"Also, it's how the brain works," Richard responds. "If people could get further into technology, they could change it."

There is a lull in the conversation, and Mike, for the first time, leans in and says confidently, "If I'm still alive on the day they cure autism, I'm not going to do it. It's who I am."

Everyone pauses, and another silence ensues. The other students nod in agreement.

"Beautifully said," I praise Mike, trying to keep the pride I am feeling for him from developing into tears of joy. I keep it cool and continue, "Mike makes a good point that autism is part of who you are. Maybe what Mike is saying, correct me if I'm wrong, is that the best parts of himself are those parts that are tied to autism. Unfortunately, often people don't see it that way."

Mike smiles broadly. The other students continue to talk about the passage, sharing their insights and connections, while Mike listens in, participating on his terms.

I share this story because it helps us think about how we can maintain and sustain book clubs in differentiated ways for our students. Mike, who is mostly nonspeaking, in this instance has asserted himself in a powerful way. He had not spoken before in our group, and today was his first verbal act. In subsequent book club sessions, Mike began to insert himself more and more—and his peers paused and gave him space to do so.

In this chapter, we will focus on maintaining and sustaining book clubs over time—*maintaining* meaning how we can create differentiated structures for book clubs and *sustaining* meaning how we can develop routines (with flexibility, of course) that nurture students' engagement in collective spaces. What are the structures for maintenance to keep supportive systems going? What is the sustenance? How do we nurture students and book clubs to continually improve our processes for collaboration and literacy growth?

For some readers, this chapter may feel classroom-centered. For those of you who are facilitating book clubs in alternative spaces, outside of the classroom, keep what you want in your pocket and don't feel pressured to use all the suggestions offered here. Throughout this journey, I will be specific about differentiating our facilitation practices to account for various book club contexts.

WHAT ARE THE STRUCTURES WE CAN USE TO MAINTAIN BOOK CLUBS?

Because our students' identities are complex and diverse and because their needs are *also* complex and diverse, it is helpful to have differentiated structures for how book clubs can function. Figure 4.1 provides various structures for book clubs so that we can ensure students are reading actively. Each structure helps with the maintenance of book club processes in that students keep track of their reading, keeping notes to bring to book club; these notes then guide

Figure 4.1. Book Club Structures

Book Club Structures	What It Is	Advantages	Disadvantages
Role Sheets	Each student takes a different role, and if you want, each week students can switch roles to try out different ways of engaging with texts.	• Provides students with a specific focus for their reading. • Scaffolds the reading process and book club discussions. • Provides clarity for how students can respond. • Offers students different ways of engaging with texts.	• Can be stifling for students. • May not allow for organic conversations during book clubs. • Facilitator-directed.
Graphic Organizers or Bookmarks	Facilitators can create graphic organizers or bookmarks that align with reading strategies and/or the content focus; the prompts can be open-ended to allow more freedom of response.		
Journals (Personal or Dialogic)	Students keep journals and respond how they want. Dialogic journals are when two students read the same book and write to each other about their reading.	• Provides flexibility in how students respond. • Allows independence and freedom.	• Does not offer as much scaffolding for reading processes.
Sticky Notes	Students keep sticky notes in their books to track their engagements as they read.		

their conversations. The role sheets, graphic organizers, and bookmarks are the most scaffolded options, whereas sticky notes and journaling offer the least amount of support and the most amount of freedom for student response and creativity. Each of these options can be offered to students in person or in digital spaces, which we will explore more in Chapter 7. When considering these options, we should ask ourselves the following: Which structure most fits our students' needs? Look back to your planning template. What are the purposes of your book clubs? Which structure will help you to sustain those goals?

Role Sheets. When I first integrated book clubs in my classroom (think back to Freddie and *The Last Vampire* book club), I provided students with role sheets. Each student within a group had a role, and each week, students would change that role so that they could try different ways of engaging with texts. For me, the role sheets have been most successful in my classroom settings, as each of the roles aligned with a reading strategy I wanted students to understand and use in authentic ways. Some of the roles we can offer students are as follows (Daniels, 2002):

- **Summarizer:** Summarizes the significant events
- **Visualizer:** Draws images of what happens
- **Literary Luminary:** Locates and analyzes significant passages
- **Connector:** Makes connections to the text, including text-to-text, text-to-self, and text-to-world
- **Questioner:** Develops critical questions
- **Word Wizard:** Locates and defines new words they don't know or identifies words they find beautiful or significant
- **Terminator:** Locates and analyzes literary terms (e.g., symbolism, simile, metaphor)

Thein, Guise, and Sloan (2011) offer other roles that allow students to try on more critical positionalities as readers, including problem poser, perspective taker, difference locator, stereotype tracker, and critical lens wearer. For examples of what these role sheets can look like, see the website, where you will also find a book club tracker to monitor the pages students are reading and the roles they enact each week. These trackers help us to see if students are on top of their reading, allowing us to support those who may be behind; they also provide reminders of the different roles students take so that they have opportunities to engage with other roles.

To scaffold role sheets, facilitators can offer students opportunities to practice these roles before diving into their book clubs. For example, a few weeks before we begin our books, I provide students with a series of thematically connected and culturally relevant short stories and poems. During this time, I model how to take on each role and then provide students with time to practice. This way, when we start book clubs, students are clear on my expectations for each role. Additionally, I celebrate student work on my classroom walls, sharing models for what the robust role sheets can look like.

I also find providing students with an agenda helpful if they need support during their book club conversations. (Note that there are seven roles—which makes for a big book club. I suggest keeping book clubs no larger than six but greater than three so that there are enough students to sustain conversations—but not too many that students feel silenced and overwhelmed.)

Sample Role Sheet Agenda (45–60 minutes)

1. Opening activity for relationship- and trust-building.
2. **Summarizer**, read your summaries. Check to see if anyone wants to add more details.
3. **Visualizer**, share your pictures. Explain what you drew and why—or have your peers guess what is happening in your images.
4. **Literary Luminary**, read each of your passages slowly, one at a time. Pause after each passage and give your peers time to comment. Share why you selected those passages and allow others to offer their insights.
5. **Word Wizard**, share the words you selected. Explain why you chose them and what the words mean literally—and what they might mean to you personally. Allow others to offer insights.
6. **Terminator**, share the literary terms you found. Explain what you think the meaning is behind these terms and why they are important. Allow others to offer their insights.
7. **Connector**, share your connections. Ask others if they made any as they read.
8. **Questioner**, read your first question. Wait for your peers to respond. Leave time for a free-flowing conversation. If people seem like they are done with this question, then move on to the next one. Perhaps start with your "juicier" questions first—the ones you think will elicit the richest discussions. Give others time to discuss—and don't worry if you don't get to all your questions!
9. Closing activity.

During my first year of book clubs, this process worked well for my students. Each group had a folder they kept in the classroom, and inside that folder were their role sheets, along with their goal sheets and their group and individual reflections.

However, I initially found that when observing book clubs, students would often simply take out their role sheets and read from them—instead of actually engaging in conversations. In one group, for example, the questioner read his list of questions instead of stopping and asking for others' responses. Thus, I created the explicit agenda above to help students engage in more authentic conversations; I also modified my role sheets to clarify their tasks for book club meetings. Simultaneously, I offered mini-lessons before students met to make their book clubs more interactive and inclusive. These are short, usually only 10–15 minutes, and address any areas where I think students can benefit, from teaching different literacy strategies to offering suggestions for conversations. I even asked three other teachers who were on break to help me model how we could have conversations using these sheets. In this case, we sat in a circle in the middle of the classroom and discussed a chapter we had all read together, modeling how to keep the conversations going and how to respond to others. In later years, I videoed students in their book clubs so I could share those as well. This level of scaffolding is critical, especially when we try new structures. These role sheets were also practical for accountability and assessments. Grading pressures are palpable, especially for classroom teachers. These sheets worked for all of those purposes, and ultimately, they worked for many book groups.

But not for all.

That first year of book clubs, after 4 weeks, Freddie asked, "Miss, do we have to do these role sheets? They get in the way. Sometimes, I want to ask questions—but then I can't because I'm the vocab guy. Maybe I don't want to be that guy."

I knew then that while choice in books was critical, so was choice in the ways we ask students to respond and engage with their reading and each other. So, that year, many of my in-class book clubs kept those role sheets because they appreciated the structure, but Freddie and his group needed more options.

Graphic Organizers and Bookmarks. As both a classroom teacher and out-of-classroom book club facilitator, I want to hold students accountable yet also provide flexibility, so I created graphic organizers. Figure 2.1 in Chapter 2 is one example of those organizers, where students have the freedom to enact four of the roles that are offered in the previous role sheets: They could write down their favorite passages (the literary luminary), collect questions (the questioner), make connections (the connector), and track their thinking, their opinions, and their thoughts as they read. If they wanted to draw in that box, they could, and if they wanted to write down vocabulary words they didn't know, they could do that as well. Compared to the role sheets, this kind of graphic organizer offered students much more freedom and flexibility for capturing their experiences with the reading.

In using these graphic organizers, however, I found a new struggle, which was that some of my students were losing them. (We often would find them smashed at the bottom of their book bags.) Simultaneously, many forgot what page they were on—and I was continually snagging bookmarks from our librarian. To alleviate both struggles, I created bookmarks on cardstock paper so that students could track what they were reading and what page they were on. According to the purpose of my book clubs and what we were focusing on, these bookmarks changed over time. For example, as a middle school social studies teacher, you might decide to use book clubs to help students understand various resistance movements, offering students five choices of nonfiction and historical fiction texts:

- *The Revolution of Evelyn Serrano* (Manzano, 2014): About the Young Lords, a Puerto Rican activist group from the 1960s
- *Claudette Colvin: Twice Toward Justice* (Hoose, 2010): About Claudette Colvin and her role during the Civil Rights movement
- *Fire in the Streets* (Magoon, 2013): About Maxie, a Black Panther, living in Chicago during the 1960s
- *When They Call You a Terrorist (Young Adult Edition): A Story of Black Lives Matter and the Power to Change the World* (Khan-Cullors & bandele, 2020): About the Black Lives Matter movement
- *The Stonewall Riots: Coming Out in the Streets* (Pitman, 2019): About the Stonewall demonstrations by members of the LGBTQ community in 1969

In using these texts, social studies teachers may have two purposes: (1) teaching students the literacy skill of retelling a sequence of historical events and (2) identifying ways in which people can advocate for themselves and others (see Figure 4.2).

Notice that this bookmark is scaffolded—offering students prompts—yet they have freedom in what passages they respond to. Simultaneously, the bookmark captures the teacher's goals of sequencing and identifying acts of resistance, while also offering a place for students to generate their questions and imagine their role within social justice work.

Like the role sheets, when using bookmarks, we might provide students with an agenda.

Sample Bookmark Agenda (45–60 minutes)

1. Opening activity for relationship- and trust-building.
2. Review your sequence of events. Share what you thought were the most important moments within the reading.
3. Taking turns, ask each other the questions that arose for you. Be sure everyone has a voice and gets a chance to both ask *and* answer questions.
4. Review your acts of resistance. Share what you noticed about activism. What did people do? What were they fighting for? What did advocacy look like?
5. Share your inspirations. What inspired you? What brought you joy? What can we learn from these acts of resistance? What could we imagine, dream, or do in our lives to emulate these leaders and community organizers?
6. Closing activity.

Figure 4.2. Sample Bookmark

Independent Reading Bookmark	Questions for My Peers

Independent Reading Bookmark

Name: _____

Title of My Book: _____

I need to read two days a week for homework. I will do this . . .

Day	Time	Location

Date Read	Pages Read
Monday In-class	
Wednesday In-class	
Homework	
Homework	

This week, during my four days of reading, the following important events happened in my book . . .

Questions for My Peers
Some questions that I want to discuss with my peers are . . .

Acts of Resistance
During my reading, I witnessed several acts of resistance, including . . .

As I read, I was most inspired by . . . and it made me think that I could . . .

On the website are other examples of bookmarks. Just keep in mind that these are templates, and that your bookmarks should reflect the literacy strategies and the content you are focusing on.

Sticky Notes and Journals. Another option is to provide students with a journal or a stack of sticky notes. In this case, students have many options for how they want to respond. Using a journal, they can respond through artwork, poetry, bullet points, and written responses. With this format, we want to set clear expectations. Perhaps explain, "I want you to fill up one page after each time you read" or "I want you to fill up one page once a week." I also provide students with sample prompts that they can tape to the front panel of their journals—or if they are using Google Docs, then I share the document below to help students when they may be stuck. These prompts are meant to be guiding questions only that allow students choice, and, of course, these prompts might change based on the purpose of your book clubs.

Sample Journal Prompts

The purpose of this journal is for you to record your thoughts as they relate to the books we are reading. Tell us what you are thinking as you read. Below are some questions you may want to respond to:

- What does the book make you think of?
- What are you learning from the book?
- How does the book make you feel?
- How does the book reflect your life?
- What kinds of things do you wonder as you read? What questions might you ask your peers?
- What does this book remind you of?
- How is the book similar to your life? How is the book different from your life?
- What character or person do you most relate to and why?
- How has this book changed your thinking?
- What about this book brings you joy or hope?
- Think about a critical event in your reading: What happened? What would you have done in this situation? What would you do differently or the same?

Try to write about your feelings and thoughts either while you are reading or immediately after reading. Anything you write here will remain confidential, between you and me. You can choose what you want to share once we are in book club.

Instead of individual journaling, students can opt to keep dialogic journals. In these spaces, students pair up and write back and forth to one another about how they are engaging with the text. They can use the same questions above to guide their responses.

Another option is to give students sticky notes. (If they are reading e-books, these are already in their e-readers.) Ask students to record personal connections or ask questions as they read. You can also give them the guiding questions that I've provided above. You can even place those prompts on a bookmark for easy access! Again, your guidance to students should be connected to the purpose of your book club and your students' needs. For my students who chose sticky notes as an option, at the end of the week I asked them to put their six favorite sticky notes on a piece of paper with their name on it. That way, I could assess weekly how they were engaging with the texts. For me, the sticky notes and the journals also worked well for my out-of-classroom book clubs as these ways of responding felt less like "homework" for students.

The agenda for this kind of book club also has a lot more freedom—and the one below is the agenda I use most frequently for my book clubs that occur outside of the classroom.

Sample Journal/Sticky Note Agenda (45–60 minutes)

1. Opening activity for relationship- and trust-building.
2. Summarize collectively the reading.
3. Discuss the reading, sharing from your journals or sticky notes.
4. Read the next section aloud (if there is time).
5. Closing activity.

There are certainly many options for students, different ways they can engage with the texts and one another. Perhaps you can also ask your students how they want to engage with the text. Do they want to use the role sheets, or would they prefer sticky notes or journals?

What I have found useful is that for 2–3 weeks before we begin book clubs, I ask students to experiment with each kind of response, using short stories and poems. For one week, they use role sheets; one week, bookmarks; and one week, sticky notes. Book club groups can then select their preferred method of response.

And to be transparent: When my book clubs were out of the classroom, where I didn't have to worry about grades, often students just read independently and came to book club ready to discuss. I did not assign bookmarks or role sheets, nor did I have students use journals or sticky notes, unless as a group or individually students felt like they needed those supports. The agenda in this case is much more informal, beginning with talking about our lives and diving into the content of the texts. Students come with their own questions and passages they want to discuss, and I am there to facilitate, participate, and enjoy the process. That being said, I always come to book club with a series of questions in case there are ever lulls in the discussions.

Our co-ed book club from Chapter 3 in the library is an example of such flexible processes. At the beginning of the year, I gave them all journals and sticky notes, and during our fourth session, Karla asked, "Do we have to use this journal or these sticky notes?"

Clifford agreed, "Yeah, miss. They kind of get in my way. I don't want this to feel like school or homework. I just wanna read and talk."

I listened to my students, and we ended up not using those tools. Except for Justine.

She loved writing, and so each week, she and I engaged in dialogic journaling. She wrote pages and pages—sometimes about the book and sometimes about her life as it connected to the texts—and then I responded back to her in writing, asking her questions and praising her thoughtfulness. Listening to students is critical if we want them to be motivated and engaged with one another in humanizing ways. This kind of flexibility is so important in sustaining students' interests and engagements with the process.

A QUICK NOTE ON TIMING

All students are different. Sometimes, it can feel like they can talk for hours about their books, and sometimes it feels like they can talk for only 5 minutes. Feel free to scaffold this timing with your students. Start small; begin with just 10-minute book clubs. Then the next week build up to 15. Continue to ratchet up this timing according to where your students are. As to the sample agendas above? Scale them down too if needed!

Now that we've looked at formats for your book club, let's return to our planning template:

Maintaining and Sustaining Book Clubs
What book club structure will you use initially? (i.e., role sheets, graphic organizers, journals, sticky notes—keeping in mind this may change based on student need) Will the whole group use these tools? Or will you allow each individual student or group to choose their method of response?
What will your agendas look like? What does a "typical" session include?

WHAT ARE THE RITUALS WE CAN USE
TO SUSTAIN OUR BOOK CLUBS?

Every book club will have its own personality, and like fingerprints, no two book clubs will ever look or sound the same. Our students are diverse and complex, as are their needs, and when they are within a group having conversations, those diverse interactions will yield very diverse perspectives. This is why being flexible is so critical as a facilitator.

Hand in hand with flexibility is holding students accountable with high expectations and differentiated scaffolding. As facilitators, we want to make sure our book clubs are progressing, that their conversations are getting more complex and that their relationships become stronger and more nuanced. Regardless of the type of book club we decide to use or the agenda we follow, we must work tirelessly to build trust and community if we want to sustain our book clubs.

This is why opening and closing activities and rituals are so important. These routines provide sustenance, ways students can build relationships with one another and reflect on improving collectively. Usually, opening activities can last 5–10 minutes, depending on what you are doing. Often, I keep it simple and use what Kay (2018) calls "Burn Five Minutes," where every time before we begin book club, I check in to see how students are feeling. I ask students a range of questions, from sharing something special that happened over the weekend to a song they feel connected to at the moment.

Topics can also address current events, especially if something important is happening in our communities. During spring 2020, for example, when schools closed due to COVID-19, I asked my students in our online book club, "What do you do to bring joy to your daily lives?"

I also might select opening questions based on what is happening in the book. For instance, one of my book clubs read *How to Make Friends With the Dark* (Glasgow, 2019), where the main character wears the same dress daily to remember her mother who has just died. I started our group by asking students if there was something in their lives that they kept to remember someone special. When asking these kinds of questions, I always try to share my own responses so that students can see me taking risks and being vulnerable as well. Hill (2009) explains that while we can never truly relinquish our power, based on the innate nature of our positionality as facilitators, our willingness to render ourselves vulnerable can dismantle and reorganize those power relations to "allow for more democratic, engaged, and productive practices" (p. 283).

Another opening ritual that I often use is to provide students with slips of paper that have quotations. These quotes are followed by optional guiding questions. Students receive different slips of paper and then write down their responses. This practice helped tremendously with my students who needed time to think before having more free-flowing conversations. Figure 4.3 is an example from *Reality Boy* (King, 2013).

Figure 4.3. Sample Opening Questions

"I can't figure out if I even care about graduation. I don't think I do. I don't think it matters. To me or anyone else. I think all anyone really cares about is that I don't get locked up. And all I care about is getting out of here. I don't really think I could go to college anyway."

What advice would you give Gerald? What would you tell him if you were his friend?

"[Special Ed] class is my mother . . . we're an accidental family."

What does Gerald mean when he says this? What does his Special Ed class mean to him? How does he feel when he is in there?

"I know from driving past the mental hospital a few miles away that people on the outside look in and just see mental patients. Not people. That's how people look at SPED too. But we're all people."

What does Gerald mean here? What is his message?

Instead of quotations, sometimes I provide students different questions so they have choices. For example, "Select one question and respond:

- What is one positive thing that happened to you this week?
- What is one thing that you are looking forward to about this weekend?
- Gerald has a group of friends he trusts in his class. What makes a good friend?
- Gerald really loves and misses his sister, Lisi. Describe a family member who you feel really close to."

Closing rituals are equally important, both to build community and to reflect on the process. Your closing rituals, usually 5–10 minutes, can be around the book, the book club process, or building relationships. Figure 4.4 offers sample questions, depending on the kind of debriefing we want students to engage in.

Ideally, we want these opening and closing rituals and questions to come from students themselves, and so once they are accustomed to our structure, I ask *them* to develop our questions: What do you need to know about your peers to have a successful book club? What are some opening and closing questions we could use to build community?

Figure 4.4. Sample Closing Questions

Sample Closing Questions on the Book	Sample Closing Questions on the Process	Sample Closing Questions for Community-Building
• What's your prediction for what will happen next in the book? • What do you hope will happen and why? • If you could change one thing about the book, a character or an event, what would it be and why?	• How did we do as a group today? • What went well for you? • What do you wish you had done differently today? • What's one new thing you learned from a peer, something that made you think differently than you were thinking before? • How did your reading of the text change after our conversations?	• What's one thing you are most excited for at the end of this day? • What's one thing you are most excited for this weekend? • What's your theme song—the song that would describe and encapsulate who you are? • Describe one thing that brings you hope and joy.

We might also want our book clubs to engage in more formalized reflective processes. For the last 5 minutes of my in-class book clubs, for example, I ask students to write up collective or individual reflections responding to the following:

Collective Reflection

- Describe the three most interesting ideas you talked about today.
- Describe three accomplishments you made as a group. What were some things you noticed people doing that helped move your book club forward?
- What is one thing that you want to improve for next time? Looking to the future, what can you do differently to improve the process?

Individual Reflection

- Describe one thing that you shared today in group.
- Describe one thing you did well today.
- Describe one thing you want to improve.

WHAT MINI-LESSONS CAN WE USE TO SUSTAIN OUR BOOK CLUBS?

In addition to providing opening and closing rituals, another way to sustain book clubs is to offer students mini-lessons based on their needs. For classroom teachers, mini-lessons may be much more formalized and structured. For out-of-classroom book clubs, mini-lessons can be more casual collaborative conversations that explicitly address ways students can progress as readers and book club members.

I offer my students two different kinds of mini-lessons: those that help their reading and those that help their discussions. Figure 4.5 offers a list of the types of mini-lessons we might provide, but they will differ, of course, according to students' needs.

These mini-lessons last between 5 and 15 minutes, where I explain *what* the strategy is, followed by *why* that strategy is important and why we need it to improve our book clubs. After direct instruction of the mini-lesson, I then model what that strategy looks like in practice.

Most importantly, we should decide the content of our mini-lessons based on student needs. Thus, careful and close observations are critical in determining what we might need to teach or review. Consider these observations *maintenance*, where we closely look at student engagements to determine the *sustenance* they need. And our *sustenance* is those mini-lessons!

One tool I use for in- and out-of-classroom book clubs is a simple table to keep track of my observations. Figure 4.6 is an example of the notes I take at the end of the day or just after a book club session.

By using this tool, I can track collectively how students are progressing with the reading while seeing the impact of my mini-lessons. I can also make notes about individual student issues. For example, Jesse had not done the reading. After class that day, I checked in with him privately to see what kind of support he needed to finish the text.

If we teach larger classes of students where several book clubs are happening simultaneously, we might use a different observational tracker (see Figure 4.7). In this case, I try to spend at least 3–5 minutes observing each group to get a sense of how they are doing. While circling the room, I try to be as noninvasive as possible to avoid interrupting student progress. For a

Figure 4.5. Sample Mini-Lessons

Sample Reading Mini-Lessons	Sample Discussion Mini-Lessons
• How to make a variety of connections • How to ask different types of questions • How to visualize • How to summarize • How to discern "significance" in reading passages: How do we know what is important? • How to make inferences	• How to listen actively • How to share air time • How to disagree constructively • How to invite students in who might be quieter • How to avoid dominating the conversation • How to keep the conversations going, especially when book club gets quiet (and awkward)

Figure 4.6. Sample Observational Notes

			Pages Read in Group	Outside Reading Goal	
Date	Attendance	Mini-Lessons			Observational Notes
2/5	Ally, Kendra, Thomas, Jesse, Elias	Kinds of questions we can ask	1–12	13–29	Some quick to judge others' responses
2/12	Ally, Kendra, Thomas, Jesse, Elias	Responding without judgment, review types of questions	30–36	36–55	Some students dominating the conversations, Jesse behind in the reading

Reality Boy (King, 2013)

Figure 4.7. Sample Observational Notes

holistic view, I simply make two columns on my paper: what is working and what could be improved.

In this example, I'm just getting a general sense of the kinds of engagements that are happening. One is an individual behavior (cell phone on lap) and another is a collective behavior (talking about a test that is coming up next period). If this method feels too informal, I've also used a more formalized checklist (see Figure 4.8).

For the last few minutes of class, I can use either the formal or the informal observational notes to share aloud with students areas where students excelled. I especially love celebrating the wonderful words that students provide to each other. While not using names directly, I praise my general noticings

Figure 4.8. Sample Observational Sheet

Book Clubs Observation Sheet

Book: *Tears of a Tiger* (Draper, 1996)

Date: December 1

Name	Prepared w/Notes	Participated in Group	Literacy Noticings	Discussion Noticings
Brenda	Y	Y	I have a friend who got really depressed like Andy.	Invited Joe's opinion
Joe	Y	Y	I didn't think the part was realistic when he went to the counselor.	Side talk with Dan about the basketball game
Mary	Y	Y	I know how you feel because my mom got depressed like that.	Eye contact
Dan	N	Y	I didn't read it.	Asked questions, still involved in conversations
Melinda	Y	N	No comments	Sat quietly

and offer direct quotations from students to demonstrate impactful ways to engage with one another. I share what I observed about their discussions, from making eye contact to asking questions. In terms of areas where I see room for improvement, I can either speak to students one to one (maybe it is a reminder to the one student with a cell phone on their lap or maybe it is checking in with Melinda to see if she is okay), or I can prepare a mini-lesson before our next book club begins. I might also decide that the following week I will sit with one or two particular book clubs who might need additional support.

Regardless of your book club or classroom size, these lessons should always come from student need. We must constantly ask ourselves: Now that I have this information, how can I provide sustenance? What nurturing do the students and book clubs need?

Let's return to the *Reality Boy* book club as an example (see Figure 4.6). My first mini-lesson was to get them to ask questions of each other. I provided students first with a handout that offered them a list of different question types, along with what they are and examples as they connected to the novel we were reading (see the website). I then asked them to practice writing these questions, which they later shared with their group. I also provided students with a bookmark of the types of questions to support them individually.

After providing the questioning mini-lesson and finishing our first meeting, I noticed that Thomas, Jesse, and Elias often judged their peers' responses in ways that would shut other students down. I spoke with all three of them individually, in private, but I also thought that we could all benefit from a collective lesson. For our second book club, we began with reviewing questions for additional practice, followed by a new lesson on how we can listen and respond to one another without judgment. Figure 4.9 is the mini-lesson I used.

After discussing these scenarios, I then provided students with a bookmark that would remind them of strategies to decrease judgments so that everyone in the group could work in intentional ways to help others feel safe and comfortable (see the website).

A QUICK NOTE ON QUESTIONING

Asking questions is often the first mini-lesson I offer, turning to queer theory scholars who ask us to focus on the questions rather than the answers (Shlasko, 2005): Whereas mainstream educators might ask, "What information shall I convey to my students?" (p. 128), a culturally sustaining educator might ask, "What questions shall we ask of each other? After we explore these questions, what will have been left out? And then what other questions shall we ask of each other?" (p. 128). These are powerful prompts to extend students' thinking.

HOW CAN WE NURTURE STUDENTS' READING OUTSIDE OF BOOK CLUB?

We've reviewed several approaches for what to do *inside* of book club, but how do we nurture students outside of our communities? The first, and most important, level of support is providing students with time and space to read. Sometimes students may not have home environments that afford these opportunities. They may share a bedroom; they may take care of siblings. One of my students, Keisha, told me she read in her bathtub with the door closed to block out the noise of the television and her family. Keeping these perspectives in mind, we need to create spaces where students can do the reading.

If you are a classroom teacher, this means providing time for independent reading during your instructional week. Remember, our daily schedule demonstrates to students what we value. Therefore, we need to provide time in class that is devoted to this critical activity. If you are not a classroom teacher but are facilitating book clubs, try to create space before or after school or during lunch. Find a quiet room in your building and make that your Independent Reading Room. You can also collaborate with classroom teachers,

Figure 4.9. Listening Mini-Lesson

Listening and Responding Without Judgment

Part One: Listening (10 minutes)

- Writing Prompt: Why is it important to listen to each other? How do you know someone is not listening to you? How do you know someone *is* listening to you?
- Discuss Responses: Take notes on chart paper of how we know someone is listening. Examples might include: We make eye contact. We nod our heads or smile. We wait to talk until the person is done talking. We respond to what the person has said.
- Practice: Have a volunteer talk about a vacation they took, a hobby, or a favorite movie or video game. The student should talk as long as possible while we practice these strategies.

Part Two: Responding Without Judgment (15 minutes)

- Writing Prompt: What does it mean to judge someone? How does that make this person feel?
- Discuss Responses: Key points might include: Everyone is judgmental! This is to be human. But we should be sensitive about our judgments in how we say them out loud. How can we not judge in our interactions with one another?
- Provide students with scenarios on slips of paper. Each student reads aloud their scenario and students discuss how to respond in nonjudgmental ways.
- Provide students with a reminder bookmark of ways we can work on this.

Scenario A

Your friend says to you, "I love waking up at 5 a.m. in the morning." You love to sleep in and hate waking up. How could you respond without judgment?

Scenario B

Your friend is going out with a person you think is really mean to others—and to you. How could you respond to your friend without judgment?

Scenario C

Someone in book club says something you don't agree with. How could you respond without judgment?

Scenario D

Someone in book club tells a story that is very personal in their life. How could you respond without judgment?

asking them to consider allowing independent reading time in their classes where students can choose to read their book club texts.

Providing independent reading during the school day is critical—and the research demonstrates that this activity is profoundly impactful. Researchers have found strong correlations between time students spend on reading and their reading development (Allington, 2014; Harvey & Ward, 2017; Krashen,

2011). The more students read, the better readers they become! The National Endowment for the Arts (2007) agrees, finding that in addition to increasing reading proficiencies, independent reading is associated with greater academic, financial, professional, and civic benefits. Similarly, independent reading builds our students' cultural and background knowledge and cultural literacies (Willingham, 2015). Independent reading also helps students develop their reading stamina and skills, including fluency, comprehension, and vocabulary (Allington, 2014; Reutzel, Petscher, & Spichtig, 2012).

In addition to offering independent reading during the day, we can support students by using various scaffolds. For emergent bi- and multilingual learners, we can sustain their reading by providing texts in their home languages. If students struggle with reading, we can offer them audio versions of the book. Sites such as www.bluford.org provide culturally relevant texts along with free audio accompaniments. Explain to students they should read the book *while* listening to build their fluency and help them be more successful with the text.

What are *we* doing while students are reading their books in our communal spaces? We can model reading by just sitting down and reading books with our students. This simple action emphasizes lifelong reading as a practice and helps to strengthen our community of readers. (This can also be a great time for you to keep up with your own reading for book club!)

As discussed in Chapter 3, I also recommend conferring with students while they are reading. We can use conferences as a way to teach or reinforce reading strategies. In the past, I've kept a log to keep track of students' reading progress (see the website). These quick check-ins with students can last anywhere from 5 to 10 minutes, depending on the level of support the student needs. The first step is to ask the reader the book's name and the page number they are on. From there, I ask readers what the book is about so far—and then have them read aloud a short portion of the text (anywhere from one paragraph to one page). Based on the reading, I follow up with a reading comprehension question, asking something specific about the passage. If necessary, I provide a mini-lesson based on what I am noticing. Before leaving the student, I ask them to set a goal for themselves and then write it on a sticky note to keep in their book. We then revisit it during our next reading conference.

WHAT ASSESSMENTS CAN WE USE TO MAINTAIN AND SUSTAIN STUDENT PROGRESS?

Traditionally, we often think about assessments as grades, as ways students can demonstrate their learning. But I want us to consider assessments as also maintenance *and* sustenance: *maintenance* in that we use them to inform our instruction and *sustenance* in that students can engage in assessments that sustain their rich linguistic and cultural diversities—that tap into their various abilities and interests. Waitoller and King Thorius (2016) encourage us to think about assessments as ongoing and flexible, both in how the information is presented and in how students perform. This section will explore how to reframe assessments both as classroom teachers and book club facilitators.

First, the great news is that we've already covered so many assessments in this chapter! Let's think about the individual assessments we've discussed and what they actually assess. Keep in mind that these are formative assessments, which tell us in an informal way how our students are doing so that (1) they can get a sense of their progress, and (2) we can use that information to guide our instruction. Figure 4.10 provides an overview of these assessments, along with the kinds of content and literacies they are assessing.

These assessments helped me, as a classroom teacher, stay on top of the collective and individual progress of my students. However, for those of you who are offering book clubs outside of class, this level of assessment is certainly not necessary. That being said, I still keep notes from all of my

Figure 4.10. Sample Formative Assessments

Formative Assessments	Content and Literacies Assessed
Role Sheets (Individual)	• Content within the text • <u>Reading Skills</u>: Summarizing, visualizing, identifying and analyzing textual evidence, making connections, asking questions, determining the meaning of words, and identifying and analyzing literary terms
Graphic Organizers (Individual)	• Content within the text • Varies based on the skills aligned with the organizer • <u>Reading Skills</u>: Identifying and analyzing textual evidence, asking questions, and making connections
Bookmarks (Individual)	• Content within the text • Varies based on the skills aligned with the bookmark • <u>Reading Skills</u>: Summarizing, determining significance and sequence of events, asking questions, and making connections
Journals and Sticky Notes (Individual)	• Content within the text • Varies based on the skills aligned with facilitator guidance • <u>Reading Skills</u>: Evaluating and analyzing the text, making connections, asking questions, and summarizing
Informal Observational Notes (Individual and Collective)	• Speaking, listening, and reading skills • Student progress in the texts • Individual and group feedback
Collective and Individual Reflections	• Speaking and listening skills • Self-evaluation

extracurricular book clubs in that I write down my noticings about the group process so that the following week I can offer mini-lessons about ways to improve our conversations and textual engagements.

But what about grading? Obviously, this is really dependent on our schools and individual styles for evaluating students. However, I know examples are helpful and so I've provided in Figure 4.11 a sample weekly evaluation form that I use for each student.

A QUICK NOTE ON INTEGRATING ASSESSMENTS

Don't feel pressured to do all these assessments at once. Figure out the level that works best for you and your students:

Level I: Take notes during or after your book clubs (most often used in out-of-classroom book clubs).

Level II: Choose one formative assessment only (used in both in- and out-of-classroom book clubs).

Level III: Select multiple assessments for a robust analysis (most often used in the classroom).

Figure 4.11. Sample Book Club Evaluation

Weekly Book Club Evaluation

Student Name: _____ Absent Days: _____

Reading (15 points)
1. Read book during independent reading time (5 points)   _____
2. Kept up with pages of group-assigned reading (5 points)   _____
3. Had book and materials every day (5 points)   _____

Written Work (10 points)
4. Filled out role sheets or graphic organizers completely (5 points)   _____
5. Kept track of dates and pages read (5 points)   _____

Group Discussion (15 points)
6. Participated in book club discussions (5 points)   _____
7. Listened and responded to others (5 points)   _____
8. Treated peers with dignity, humility, and respect (5 points)   _____

Total Points _____/40   Overall Grade: _____

Individual Feedback:

Student Response to Feedback:

You can change this sample evaluation based on your preferences, but I offer this model to demonstrate that we need to be clear about how we grade students. It's also important for students to not just look at their grades but to actually reflect on them, and so once they get their weekly feedback from me, I give them time to respond. Maybe they disagree and we need to have a conversation. Perhaps they are proud of their performance. Or maybe they want to reflect on their improvement and thus use this space to consider their own development as readers and collaborators. From this perspective, assessments are less about grades and more about authentic reflections for growth.

Thus far, all of the assessments explained have been formative, ways for students to get ongoing feedback about their progress and ways for facilitators to decide how to nurture book clubs. But what about our summative assessments? What happens when students are done reading their books?

Well, the first thing to do is celebrate!

Finishing a book and talking collectively about it for a sustained amount of time is a big accomplishment, and thus, we want to praise students for their hard work, their courage, and their efforts.

For classroom teachers, you may decide that in addition to formative assessments you want students to engage in performance- or project-based summative assessments, assessments that are culturally sustaining and that allow students to combine their knowledge of the texts along with their diverse cultures, languages, and literacies. Like other facets of the book club process, we want to offer choice in the ways students share what they've learned through reading the texts and engaging with one another.

Below are various summative assessments we can offer. Note that all of the presentations I have suggested are done in small groups, the reason being that I want students to talk to each other about the books they read—to inspire each other to read new books, to make connections, and to see patterns and themes across different texts. I also don't want these to be individual presentations where we passively listen to each and every one as a class. These are all done collaboratively, in groups, so that students can continue to learn and interact with one another.

Book Club Jigsaws. As a book club group, give students time to create a shared presentation. Students can choose their preferred genres: perhaps a poster, a PowerPoint presentation, or a Google Slides presentation. Offer choice in how students want to "present" their book. My general recommendations are to have students

- summarize the text (without giving away the ending),
- provide an overview of the major characters or people highlighted in the book,

- share what they believe to be the author's purpose in writing the text (the major themes and big ideas), and
- offer an evaluation (what they thought of the text).

If you had a specific purpose for your book club, then they might talk about that as well. For example, if you are a middle school social studies teacher, you might have students share the significant moments of advocacy and resistance that occurred in their texts.

These presentations should be about 5 minutes long and should be engaging for others. Once the collective project is complete, I put students into new groups—with a representative from a different book in a small group of 3–6 students. During this time, students present, while their peers listen, take notes, and ask questions. The idea is to expose students to different books so that they can be inspired to read new texts in the future. In doing so, we position students "as experts of their own practices to mediate learning" (Waitoller & King Thorius, 2016, p. 382); these kinds of presentations can further offer students opportunities to represent themselves and what they've learned. On the website is a sample note-taking guide for the jigsaws.

Facebook, Instagram, or Yearbook Representations. Within groups, students can decide whether they want to create a Facebook page or Instagram account representing the events in their books. Perhaps they have read *With the Fire on High* (Acevedo, 2019), which is the narrative of Emoni Santiago, an Afro-Latinx high school senior from Philadelphia who has tremendous talents in cooking and aspirations of being a chef, all while raising her daughter. Students could create a Facebook page of Emoni, either digital or paper, where they share significant evidence and critical inferences from the text. They can find pictures and write captions of events as they connect to the story. They can fill her "wall" with updates on what she has been doing. They can also check her into places she has visited, and they can fill out her information page, sharing who her friends and family are.

Students could do the same for Emoni using Instagram, where they find photographs or even take their own photographs of different places Emoni and her friends and family have been, using captions to capture these significant events. Another option is to create a yearbook where students provide visuals and overviews of the major characters.

Once students finish their creative pieces, they can share them with other book clubs. Members of the book clubs listen and try to "piece together" what the book is about—what the main ideas were and how they may overlap with their own texts. The only "big no-no" in this project, as with all projects, is never to give away the ending.

Readers' Theater. For this summative assessment, book club members write a script of a pivotal scene in their book. They begin their scripts by summarizing overall what the text is about—the main characters and significant plot events—and then collectively act out a scene that captures the essence of their text. These are performed in front of the class and can be an extraordinary motivator for getting their peers to read their books.

Poetry Slam. Using significant lines from the texts, students write a series of "found poems," where they write poetry based on the words in the text. These poems can be shared within the space of a poetry slam—or students can create digital poems, where they put their writing in a PowerPoint or Google Slides presentation with images and music.

Action Research Roundtables. Based on the content of the texts read in book clubs, group members can collaboratively research events that occurred in their text. In addition to the research, students can create ideas for actions to support others in their communities. For example, one book club finishes *The Astonishing Color of After* (Pan, 2019), which is about a biracial female who visits her grandparents in Taiwan after her mother commits suicide. This book club might decide to conduct research on suicide prevention and create a schoolwide suicide prevention plan. Another group perhaps reads *The Love and Lies of Rukhsana Ali* (Khan, 2019), which is the story of Rukhsana, an adolescent Bengali female who is in love with another girl. When her parents find out, they move her to Bangladesh for an arranged marriage. This group might decide to research LGBTQ Muslim communities and arranged marriages. Their action research might be to create a plan for parent-teen support groups where families have opportunities to engage with each other. Students can present their research and action plans with PowerPoint or Google Slides, or classic posters or papers. Ultimately, students will share their research and action plans in jigsaw formats with other book clubs.

Children's Books. In this final example, students re-create their text into a children's book—either digitally or on paper. In previous years when I have done this, we have collaborated with local elementary schools, where students share their books with younger classrooms. During the creative processes, my students and I discuss content and language that might be more developmentally appropriate for elementary readers, strategizing ways we can modify our young adult books so that they are better suited for younger audiences.

The options are truly endless when assessing students. We want to offer them diverse methods for demonstrating their knowledge and experiences in ways that match their creativities, literacies, and languages. Simultaneously we need to be clear about our expectations, offering models, rubrics, and checklists which are helpful in guiding them through the processes.

Let's pause and plan for now. In the following chapters, we will dig into the kinds of conversations students might have during our book clubs. We will look specifically at how students can develop their literacy strategies while also focusing on social and emotional growth.

Maintaining and Sustaining Book Clubs	
What opening rituals will you use?	What are some closing rituals?
What mini-lessons might you teach? (process or literacy based)	
How can you support students' independent reading? (in or out of class)	
Assessing Students	
What ongoing formative assessments might you use?	What will you do when students finish their books? What summative assessments might you use? How will you celebrate their success?

CHAPTER 5

Developing Literacies and Spaces for Emotional and Identity-Based Engagements

It is June 2020, and our students have been working from remote spaces for the first three months of the pandemic. I am meeting with Aliyah, Niesha, Denise, and Raga. These young women have chosen to read *With the Fire on High* (Acevedo, 2019) for their book club as they all share a common love of cooking for their families. The school counselor and I begin today's session with a quotation from the book, where the main character, Emoni, a Latina adolescent, receives praise about her cooking from her abuela: "'Buela says it's definitely a blessing, magic. That my food doesn't just taste good, it *is* good—straight up bottled goodness that warms you and makes you feel better about life."

Our school counselor asks the young women how they think this comment made Emoni feel, and they respond with "grateful," "happy," and "proud." I then ask them to share something they've been told that is positive.

"I've been told I give good advice," shares Niesha. "I know just what to say in the right moment."

"Yup, that's true," smiles Raga. "You do give good advice. For me, my grandma says I could do anything in the world if I set my mind to it."

Aliyah, new to our group, a recent immigrant from Egypt who has only been in the United States for one year, shares, "Me? Cooking too. Like Emoni. One day, I make food from my country for you."

"Please do!" says Denise encouragingly. "I can't wait until all this is over! For me? My teachers say I'm good at art and that I'm mature for my age."

"These are all lovely compliments that we receive from people around us," I respond. "When students tell me that I'm a good teacher, it makes me feel good about myself and what I do. It helps my self-esteem. What do we mean when we say 'self-esteem'?"

The young women share their ideas about the concept and how it connects to Emoni and their own lives. Mostly, they discuss outside praise—and how others can make us feel good about ourselves.

"How can we build self-esteem *within* ourselves, I wonder?" I ask them. "Do we always need others to make us feel good? Do you think Emoni has a positive self-image? How do you think she builds that up?"

Collaboratively, the young women discuss Emoni and how she keeps her positive self-image, by believing in herself, by engaging in hobbies like cooking, by keeping herself surrounded by people who love her, and by being driven to support her child and care for her abuela. During this time, the young women interject pieces of themselves into the conversations, comparing their identities and lived experiences to Emoni, sharing ways they try to sustain their own self-esteem.

"I'm from Jamaica," explains Niesha. "I love my country. I am proud of who I am, and how I talk, and my friends there and my family. It makes me strong and it makes me believe in myself and who I am."

In these conversations, the character of Emoni serves as a springboard for conversations about our own identities and sense of self; simultaneously, Emoni serves as a safety net for when the young women may not want to share pieces of themselves. When facilitating book clubs, we must provide young people with choices to use the books either as springboards for sharing or as safety nets when they do not feel comfortable revealing personal aspects of themselves.

In the next two chapters, we will explore scenarios such as these to see what book clubs can look and sound like in action. In this chapter, we will focus on using book clubs to center students' literacy growth while simultaneously allowing thoughtful and intentional time for emotional and identity-based engagements. Often, educational and youth development professionals see social-emotional learning as a separate entity from our academic pursuits, but book clubs can offer a unique space to support students in both areas. In just this short anecdote, we can see how the young women summarize the text and make inferences about the main character; simultaneously, they make powerful connections to Emoni, sharing their own strategies for positive self-image and identity work. In this chapter, we will look at ways we can support young people—to build their literacies—while also centering their emotional and identity-based growth.

WHAT DO WE MEAN BY LITERACY DEVELOPMENT?

Often, we conflate literacy with just reading, as if literacy and reading are synonymous. However, literacy is much more than reading; it is our ability to write, communicate, speak, listen, and view. These skills are intertwined and help youth engage with their sense of self and their communities and the larger world. In this section, we will dig deep into students' reading and how we can develop that skill through the use of book clubs.

Some of you may be thinking, "But I'm not a reading teacher." Many of us may feel uncomfortable with reading instruction, especially if we don't have degrees in reading or literacy. But remember: Book clubs serve many purposes, so facilitators should not feel pressured to teach reading if they don't feel equipped for that work. Sometimes, we have book clubs that are just about the content—and not about reading strategies. However, if we are interested in dipping our toes into reading instruction—or even diving fully into the deep end—we might look at some research-based practices that exist to support students' comprehension.

The first myth that we must dispel is that there are *no* "best practices" for our students when considering reading instruction. Each student is unique and therefore will need different modes of instruction and different levels of scaffolding when it comes to developing their reading. That being said, we can, as facilitators, lean into recent research about teaching reading to be more informed about the ways we can help our students develop as readers. Below are a few instructional strategies we can implement during our book club sessions with students.

Word Study. Vocabulary development plays a fundamental role in reading comprehension (Roskos & Neuman, 2014); the size of students' vocabulary is strongly related to their reading proficiencies (Stahl & Nagy, 2006). As facilitators, then, perhaps consider time and space for that work. When I facilitate book clubs, especially when working with emergent bi- and multilingual learners, I try to spend about 5–10 minutes talking about new words or concepts students will encounter in their reading. For example, *Darius the Great Is Not Okay* (Khorram, 2018) is a rich fictional text about a Persian adolescent male, Darius, who is coping with depression and trying to attain a sense of belonging with his friends and family. In the first chapter, the word "calamity" arises. I might spend some time with that word, asking students, "What does calamity mean? What can you guess based on the context around that word?" Then as a group, we can develop a definition together or use our online dictionaries to help.

We might talk then about the word in the context of the book. What calamities is Darius facing? How does he work to overcome them? And if students feel comfortable sharing, they might discuss their own calamities. In this way, we are building students' vocabulary while also centering some of the emotional issues the text brings up and that students might be grappling with. Most importantly, we can collaboratively talk about ways to handle stressful events in our lives, thus paying simultaneous attention to emotional-based learning and reading development.

While I may come to book club prepared with words that I think are essential, it is also important to allow youth to share their own engagement with words. We might ask, "What words didn't you know or understand? What strategies did you use to figure out what those words mean? What words did you find beautiful or 'pocket worthy'—meaning words that you want to keep and carry with you or words that were important to the story?"

We might even ask these kinds of questions as part of our opening rituals: "What word or words stuck with you as you read? Take some time to flip through your book. Then let's all share our word and why we selected it." This is a simple way to develop vocabulary with no degree in reading necessary.

Humanizing Close Reading. When I speak to close reading, I am not referring to the close reading discussed in the Common Core (Coleman & Pimentel, 2012), which tends to disregard the rich cultural and linguistic assets our students bring to texts. When I speak to close reading, I am referring to a more humanizing approach that draws on students' funds of knowledge and lived experiences (Handsfield & Valente, 2021). In this way, students are invited to bring themselves to the reading (Muhammad & Haddix, 2016; Santori & Belfatti, 2017) and are encouraged to engage in affective and emotional responses as these feelings intersect with the text (Eppley, 2019; Wender, 2017). When we engage in close reading, we use texts that are relevant to students, allowing them to take the lead in their interpretations and subsequent conversations. We are also emotionally present, meaning as facilitators we are both vulnerable and open to our reactions—as we want our students to be as well.

Close reading is also about having students engage in multiple readings for different purposes (Lehman & Roberts, 2013). Research suggests that rereading a text can increase students' comprehension (Rawson, Dunlosky, & Thiede, 2000). I use this strategy frequently to reinforce the importance of close reading and to collectively discuss passages that focus on critical issues as they connect to students' emotional or identity development. Reading aloud—either by facilitator or students—is also a great way to increase fluency, which is a reader's ability to read words accurately, quickly, and with expression (Malmgren & Trezek, 2009). For students who may be emergent readers, for those who may be learning a new language, or for those with disabilities, building fluency is critical in that youth can then spend less time on decoding words and more time on deeper textual understandings (Boardman, Roberts, Vaughn, Wexler, Murray, & Kosanovich, 2008).

For example, *The Black Flamingo* (Atta, 2020) is a beautifully written narrative poem that captures the life of Michael, a mixed-race gay teen who lives in London. Students in our book club may read the chapter "Barbies and Belonging" on their own but when we come together, I might read this chapter aloud again. Before reading, I give students a purpose: "Let's reread 'Barbies and Belonging.' As we read, think about the gender norms Michael is experiencing. What is society saying to him, and how does that contradict his own gender identity?" As with word study, we focus on rereading a text as an instructional strategy while discussing critical issues around gender and sexuality.

As facilitators, we can also ask students to share, and reread, particular passages that speak to them. This could be another ritual within our book clubs. We might ask our students, "What passage resonated with you this week in your reading? Read it aloud and talk about why you selected this passage." This choice provides students with the power to select and discuss passages that are important to them and connect to their own lived experiences.

Explicit Reading Instruction. Explicit reading instruction involves three phases:

1. **Facilitator modeling and direct instruction,** where we teach and discuss the reading strategy and demonstrate how to use it in the context of the text
2. **Guided practice,** where the facilitator or students read the text aloud and then try out the reading strategy
3. **Independent practice,** where students read on their own and try out the reading strategy

This approach to reading instruction can increase students' comprehension and help them become independent readers who can later transfer those strategies to other areas in life and school (Marchand-Martella & Martella, 2013; National Institute for Literacy, 2007). If you are a classroom teacher, you might do this work in a more formalized way, where you project the text onto a screen for students to see your modeling. However, as an out-of-classroom facilitator, this process can be much more casual so that your book clubs don't begin to feel like "class."

So, what can this process look like in practice? A wonderful illustrated memoir titled *Almost American Girl* (Ha, 2020) tells the true story of Chuna (Robin) Ha, who comes to the United States and struggles to maintain her relationship with her mother while also adjusting to a new language and culture in her middle school in Alabama. My purpose for teaching this book is literacy-based, to teach students how to read a new genre of graphic novels. It is also emotional and identity-based, to address issues that immigrant youth may face when coming to a new country and to discuss how we can sustain and nurture our familial relationships. My first mini-lesson and modeling might demonstrate how to read a graphic novel. Looking at the first two pages, I might provide direct instruction about which direction we can read, how to interpret drawings and how to read captions. I would read and think aloud, stopping and asking for questions to make sure students understood the formatting of graphic novels.

From there, we might transition to guided practice. I would ask students to consider carefully how they make sense of the chapters, using my mini-lesson; simultaneously, I might give students a purpose in their reading, asking, "Think about Chuna's relationship with her mother as we read. Also, think about Chuna's experience during her first week in Alabama. How is she feeling?" As a group, we would then read the chapter together, stopping frequently to check for understanding while focusing on issues of relationship-building and immigration. Our independent practice would then be for students to read the second chapter on their own before our next book club.

We can also provide students with choice, offering more open-ended questions. I might ask, "As we read this chapter, think about some of the most important themes of the text. What do *you* think is important about this memoir? Why might Ha be writing it?" Then students can discuss what matters to them rather than what we have predetermined *for* them.

Ultimately, when it comes to students' reading development, we should select reading strategies based on students' needs. Reading comprehension is tricky and complex, as students' comprehension is based not only on their *background knowledge* and motivation, but also on the *text* itself and the *context*, where the reading takes place. The wonderful aspect of book club is that we can create spaces that allow for greater ease in comprehension; we are prioritizing students' interests by allowing them choice in the text, which enhances their motivation; simultaneously, we are creating a context (book club) that can be a safe forum for them to discuss elements of the text and their identities.

This all being said, there are some important cognitive strategies that we *can* teach students explicitly that will help them to develop as readers. Some of these reading strategies include activating prior knowledge, making connections, summarizing, monitoring our reading, asking questions, inferring, analyzing, and evaluating. We will discuss these more specifically later in this chapter. For now, let's pause and return to our template. Think about your students' assets when it comes to reading and then make a list of their needs. What instructional strategies can you then integrate to support them?

Supporting Students' Reading Comprehension	
What are your students' strengths in reading? What support do they need?	Which reading instructional strategies can you use to support your students?

WHAT DOES IT MEAN TO ENGAGE IN EMOTIONAL AND IDENTITY-BASED WORK?

Social-emotional learning (SEL) has been a hot topic for the last 2 decades in schools across the United States. However, James Comer, known as the grandfather of SEL, has practiced and researched these approaches since the 1960s, combining academics with social-emotional development (Comer, 2005; Panjwani, 2011). Since then, his work has created a legacy, particularly for CASEL, the Collaborative for Academic, Social, and Emotional Learning.

According to the CASEL website (2020), SEL is a process where youth "acquire and apply knowledge, skills, and attitudes to develop healthy identities, manage emotions and achieve personal and collective goals, feel and show empathy for others, establish and maintain supportive relationships, and make responsible and caring decisions." Ongoing research has demonstrated that by focusing on SEL, we can improve students' well-being while also supporting their academics (Education Trust, 2020).

While this work at its base level may seem sound, much critique has arisen, particularly from practitioners and scholars of color, who question the integrity and purpose of such work. One of the most significant flaws is that SEL comes from a place of "competence"—looking at youth gaps and deficits—instead of centering their assets. Further, the Education Trust website (2020) explains that "While all students could benefit from meaningful social-emotional supports, the students typically being discussed are students of color, students from low-income backgrounds, and English learners, who are already the targets of stereotypes about race and socioeconomic status." Many thus worry that SEL is being used as a tool for policing and oppression of marginalized populations (Abolitionist Teaching Network, 2020; Kaler-Jones, 2020). Another inherent problem is that often SEL approaches are grounded in "white, cisgender, patriarchal norms and values which further enact emotional and psychological violence onto Black, Brown, and LGBTQ youth of color" (Kaler-Jones, 2020, para. 2). In this way, SEL positions marginalized youth as "at-risk," using problematic tools to label, sort, and rank students (Strong & McMain, 2020). Critics also speak to how traditional SEL fails to address larger sociopolitical contexts and ignores inequities in students' lives (Education Trust, 2020; Simmons, 2019). Dismissing systemic injustices can be harmful to students who are already underserved in that schools are not addressing the influence of learning environments and systems that create and sustain inequities.

In response to these issues, scholars and practitioners have redefined ways we can engage with SEL. Kaler-Jones (2020), for example, asks us to consider "cultural-affirming emotional learning," as this approach centers students' cultural and linguistic diversities while also allowing spaces for "recognizing and addressing trauma" (para. 5). Similarly, Strong and McMain (2020) propose SEL for social-emotional justice (SEL-SEJ), which disrupts traditional and oppressive aspects of SEL, instead centering reciprocal, relational, and Indigenous models for learning. Abolitionist SEL is another way in which to reimagine how we approach social-emotional development; according to the Abolitionist Teaching Network website (2020), by integrating practices that are "critical, healing centered, reciprocal in nature, culturally responsive, transformative, and dialogical," we ultimately create communities that allow for both vulnerability and joy.

In the previous section, we focused on infusing reading instruction into our book clubs; now, we will continue that work, this time exploring how we can also focus on students' emotional literacies and identity development. Using the CASEL framework while centering the scholarship of culturally affirming, healing-centered, and justice-oriented SEL (Ginwright, 2018; Simmons, 2019, 2020a, 2020b), I will offer asset-based lenses for how we can position book clubs not as spaces to "fix" behaviors but as spaces to create forums where students use texts and each other to work on literacy and emotional and identity-based development. In this way, book club facilitators can focus on students' emotional health—not seeking to treat "symptoms" but to enhance their well-being by providing experiences for healing and self-care (Simmons, 2020c).

Even facilitators who do not have backgrounds in mental health can still engage in the process. Remember that bibliotherapy, which I mentioned in the first chapter, is the use of texts to help youth grapple with a myriad of issues. While social workers, counselors, psychiatrists, and psychologists can conduct *clinical bibliotherapy* as an intervention, this chapter uses elements from *developmental bibliotherapy,* which is more preventive and collective, and thus can be utilized by teachers, librarians, parents, or other school personnel. We will look at three areas we can focus on within book clubs to address students' emotional and identity-based development.

1. Cultivating Self-Awareness and Identity Development. Before diving into what we mean by self-awareness and identity development, we must return to culturally sustaining practices, which position our students' cultures as dynamic, fluid, multilayered, and evolving, based on such elements as race, ethnicity, class, ability, sexuality, gender, language, religion, immigration status, and youth culture (Ladson-Billings, 2014; Paris & Alim, 2014). Books can offer compelling representations of youth from various intersectional identities that our students may connect with and learn from. Thus, book clubs can be a place where students focus on who they are by connecting with the characters and engaging in storytelling. Personal and collective storytelling can be a powerful way in which youth share their stories of pain and resistance, while also engaging in healing processes and exploring new possibilities for hope. In particular, conversations around race, ethnicity, and identity are critical in helping students develop strong racial-ethnic identities, which are crucial for youth of color (Education Trust, 2020). The same can be said for students with dis/abilities or emergent bi- and multilingual youth, where students can speak to both their strengths and vulnerabilities, articulating aspects of their identities through positive, asset-based lenses.

When speaking of healing, we cannot expect youth to resolve all their struggles as they relate to their identities and emotions. Healing is an ongoing process, where youth can engage with and learn from the texts and one another, to discuss and negotiate strategies for well-being and self-care in a collective and reflective way (Hill, 2009).

Understanding who we are and where we fit in is critical for identity development and self-awareness (Simmons, 2019). But self-awareness can also include the ability to understand our emotions, thoughts, and values and how they influence our behaviors and how we interact with others (CASEL, 2020; Simmons, 2019). Thus, we can use texts to see how characters work through their emotions and engage with others. Self-awareness can also be about helping youth create stronger growth mindsets where they build their capacity to recognize and use their assets and strengths, as those pertain to their cultural and linguistic diversities and their various abilities.

I'll Be the One (Lee, 2020) is a wonderful example of a text with a protagonist who believes in herself and her talents. Identifying as a bisexual Korean American, Shin Haneul, or Skye, grapples with expectations from her parents and from her Korean and U.S. communities. Lee's narrative speaks to being the only Asian female in her LGBTQ Students Association and what it is like to be "fat-shamed" by everyone from her peers to her parents. Internally, Shin struggles with all of the pressures, but by surrounding herself with a strong community and using self-love exercises, she enters the world of K-Pop and breaks all stereotypes.

To engage in self-awareness and identity-based conversations, we might come to this book club with the following questions:

- What are Shin's multiple identities? (What are some of your identities?)
- What are the various emotions she experiences when she engages with her mother? (How might you feel if you were Shin?)
- How would you describe Shin's self-esteem? How does she maintain that strong sense of self? (What do you do to help boost your own sense of self?)

In these few examples, students can discuss Shin's character and her intersectional identities and how she works to maintain a growth mindset. As readers, students are engaging simultaneously with reading development, identifying important evidence from the text, making connections, and drawing inferences. The questions in parentheses then ask students to think about ways they intersect with the text. These are questions that students can choose to respond to—or they can use the safety net of just discussing Shin.

A final piece of self-awareness within book club spaces can examine our own assumptions and biases. This work can be incredibly poignant for young white students, who may not have confronted their own sense of privilege and power as it relates to their race and position in society. Reading books such as *All American Boys* (Reynolds & Kiely, 2015) might be useful in starting this work. Here, one of the main characters, Quinn, comes to understand his white identity and privilege. This text can thus be used as a model for white students to engage in self-reflection and critical self-analysis, considering their role in working for racial justice. Simmons (2019) urges us to help students "interrogate their power and privilege, as well as racism, homophobia, sexism, and other forms of violence, to consider what changes they can make within themselves and their world to achieve more equity" (para. 9). When students recognize their positionalities as they connect to social inequities, they achieve deeper understandings of themselves and of critical stances, thus beginning to imagine taking on new roles and engaging in equity-based work (Caraballo & Lyiscott, 2020).

2. Developing Emotional Literacies and Self-Care.

2. Developing Emotional Literacies and Self-Care. Emotional literacies encompass our abilities to recognize, understand, handle, and express our emotions. This work might include developing coping skills for stress and anxiety or building motivations and self-confidence. These are all difficult actions, especially for adolescents; reading texts and talking to peers with a focus on emotional literacies may be an effective way for students to address their feelings and integrate self-care strategies. Research demonstrates that when students understand their emotions, they are more motivated and equipped to develop strong relationships; further, emotional literacy can influence students' concentration, memory, and problem-solving skills while also promoting creativity, innovation, and leadership (Sharp, 2001). Emotions can also be a direct and powerful pathway for youth to develop their critical consciousness (Lorde, 2007). Morrell (2008) explains that students cannot be "informed or empowered consumers of social collectives" until they are "self-actualized" and have "begun the process of healing and loving themselves" (p. 180).

When thinking about emotional literacies, however, we must return to Kaler-Jones's (2020) skepticism that this kind of SEL might be grounded in white, cisgender, patriarchal, and able-bodied norms. Developing emotional literacies should not be about students conforming or constricting their identities—nor should students not feel free to express their "fullest, most authentic selves" (Kaler-Jones, 2020, para. 2). Developing emotional literacies can be much less deficit-oriented and more asset-based, meaning that students recognize and respond internally to their feelings and then develop coping skills for dealing with those various emotions. We might pose the following questions:

- When we are feeling sad, what methods can we use to address those feelings?
- When we're feeling unmotivated to write our college applications or apply for a job, where might that hesitation stem from and how can we set goals for ourselves?
- When we are feeling stressed and anxious about something in the news, how can we address those emotions and use them for transformation and justice?

As facilitators, we want to create spaces where students can respond to these kinds of questions and actually *feel* those feelings—spaces where they can express their emotions, whether it is rage or frustration, joy or excitement.

Often, educational and youth development professionals want to stifle feelings such as rage—however, "righteous anger has long been used as a tool to fuel movements that have and continue to propel our nation forward toward justice. To tell students to not harness their anger is to tell them their rage isn't warranted" (Kaler-Jones, 2020, para. 12).

Let's now look at an example. Historically set during the "War Between the States," *Dread Nation* (Ireland, 2018) is an action-packed, justice-oriented science fiction text that tells the story of Jane, a young Black female, who is training as a warrior against zombies. For years, science fiction writers of color from Octavia Butler to Nnedi Okorafor have utilized fantastic worlds to bring light to current injustices. Ireland does the same; unveiling issues around the intersectionalities of being female and Black, she exposes systemic racism and its impact on Native and Black peoples in the United States and obliterates any notion that a woman cannot fight—physically, emotionally, intellectually—to get justice.

Jane experiences a range of emotions from rage to sadness to insecurity. These literary moments can be places for youth to discuss how she handles and expresses those feelings, depending on her context. Jane also uses a variety of coping skills for her anxiety, which can be discussed in book club. We might then ask these questions:

- In the face of racism and sexism, how does Jane maintain her sense of self-confidence?
- How does Jane channel her emotions to resist patriarchal and racist peoples and systems?

We could also participate in close reading, focusing on compelling passages that address Jane's feelings. For example, in one of the final battles, Jane tells the lead antagonist, "See, the problem in this world ain't sinners, or even the dead. It is men who will step on anyone who stands in the way of their pursuit of power. Luckily there will always be people like me to stop them" (p. 435).

Passages such as these offer students opportunities to discuss the characters' emotional literacies. In doing so, we work to develop students' reading by identifying critical passages and analyzing them while also discussing the characters' emotional development. As facilitators, we can also connect the text and students' lived experiences, if they are comfortable with sharing. Perhaps ask students to discuss a time when they experienced frustration or rage. We might ask:

- What happened? What did you do?
- Would you have done anything differently?
- What are some ways we can care for ourselves when these feelings arise?
- How can we channel those emotions into justice-based actions?

Collaboratively, then, students can use each other to engage with their emotions, to center their intersectional identities, and work toward collective self-care.

3. Engaging in Informed Decision Making. Every day, we make decisions, small and large, that impact us in minimal and significant ways. Part of culturally affirming and justice-oriented SEL is helping students engage in informed decision making, which is our ability to take in and evaluate information and emotions to make sound, constructive decisions that are considerate of both our well-being and the well-being of others (Simmons, 2019). Informed decision making involves seeing both the benefits and the consequences of our actions and how they impact ourselves and others. Informed decision making also requires that we keep open minds and consider alternatives so that we can begin to see how we can make changes within ourselves and our communities (Simmons, 2019).

One way to help students think about making informed decisions is through graphic organizers. Graphic organizers are effective, visual tools that can be used to develop both reading skills and emotional literacies. Further, they can help students identify, organize, and analyze key points from their reading, ultimately enhancing students' comprehension (Marchand-Martella, Martella, Modderman, Petersen, & Pan, 2013). They can also be a terrific way to help students engage in conversations about complex ideas and events.

Figure 5.1 is a sample graphic organizer for helping students with their reading (i.e., identifying key plot events and cause and effect relationships and making inferences) while also helping youth think about decisions characters make and how they impact the characters around them. As an example, in *The Absolutely True Diary of a Part-Time Indian* (Alexie, 2009), Junior grows up and lives on the Spokane Reservation. Junior must decide whether to remain at his current school on the reservation or attend an all-white high school in a small farm town. Students can use this organizer to think about the dilemma Junior is experiencing. What decision does he come to—and what informed that decision? Once Junior makes that decision, how does it continue to impact him and those around him, including his family and friends? If students feel comfortable, they can also use this graphic organizer to discuss a decision that they will make in the future—or to talk about one they made in the past. In doing so, they can receive feedback from their peers and discuss how we make decisions and how those decisions impact others in our lives.

Now that we've discussed three different ways we can support students through emotional and identity-based engagements, let's return to our planning template and think about our students' assets and ways in which we can support their emotional literacies while also focusing on their intersectional identities. What might you center? What tools and questions might you integrate based on your students' needs and the textual content? Again, this is just a plan, which ultimately can and *should* change based on your students' needs as they engage with the texts and one another.

Figure 5.1. Informed Decision Making Graphic Organizer

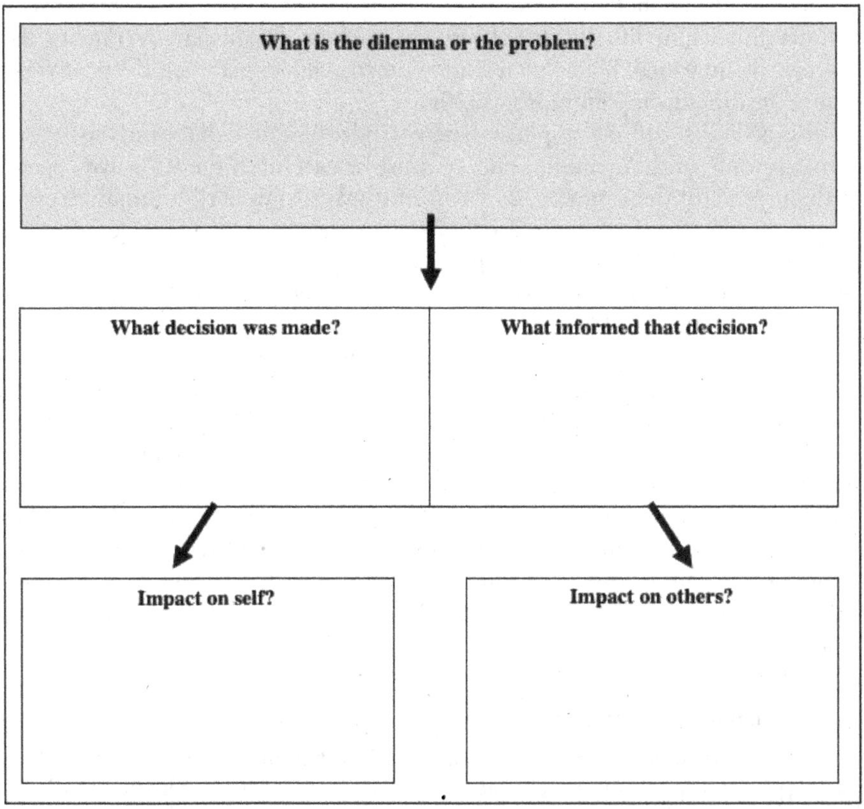

HOW CAN WE ADDRESS TRAUMA WITHIN OUR BOOK CLUBS?

Trauma is real, and it impacts our students in significant ways. Youth are impacted by personal, current, and generational trauma. Our schools can be places of trauma as well: our hallways, curriculum, and policies. Students of color, students who identify as LGBTQ, immigrant students, and students with various dis/abilities may experience trauma on a daily basis that goes unnoticed and unaddressed.

Trauma is dangerous for our students as it can cause short- and long-term effects such as anxiety and depression, decreased engagement in school, increased health problems, and difficulties in attention, reasoning, long-term memory, and reading abilities (Center on the Developing Child at Harvard University, 2016; Wade, Shea, Rubin, & Wood, 2014). Trauma can also lead to violent behaviors, suicidal tendencies, and drug abuse (Park & Schepp, 2015). Specifically, for Black, Indigenous, and people of color (BIPOC), their needs in schools historically and currently tend to go unrecognized and un-treated (Lindsey, Sheftall, Xiao, & Joe, 2019). BIPOC students who witness trauma either individually or collectively, such as the media coverage of the killings of unarmed Black men and women, can experience deep adverse mental health effects (Simmons, 2020c).

Book clubs can be a place where students can collaboratively work through some of that trauma, but we must be careful in the ways we engage with students in these spaces, as we do not want to ever re-traumatize them (Simmons, 2019). If students do choose to speak to their lived experiences, it is important that we provide spaces where they can safely and gradually begin to share at their own pace. We should also remember that youth are not just their trauma—and that book clubs can be a wonderful outlet for young people to imagine, dream, and hope (Ginwright, 2018).

What does this mean for us as book club facilitators? We must leave room for joy. We can do this by allowing choice in what students want to read and how they want to discuss those texts as this puts the power in their hands. Also, we must be prepared for difficult conversations that may arise and have resources available. This means communicating and collaborating with our students' families and working with the social workers and coun-selors within our school communities, letting them know about the conver-sations students are having so that they are there to additionally support students if necessary.

Supporting Students' Emotional Literacies and Identity Development		
What are your students' strengths and assets when thinking about their emotional development (i.e., self-awareness, identity development, emotional literacies, self-care strategies, informed decision making)? Where do students need support?		
What strategies, tools, and questions can you use to support students' self-awareness and identity development?	What strategies, tools, and questions can you use to support students' emotional literacies and self-care strategies?	What strategies, tools, and questions can you use to support students in making informed decisions?

HOW DO WE SIMULTANEOUSLY ADDRESS READING DEVELOPMENT ALONG WITH EMOTIONAL AND IDENTITY-BASED WORK?

Now that we've looked at approaches for infusing reading instruction with emotional and identity-based work into book clubs, let's look deeper into how we can marry these two goals. The connection between identity and literacy is complex in that students' identities impact how they make meaning. Similarly, the reading itself can impact students' identities; thus, a reciprocal process ensues where readers can consider the following:

- How does my identity shape the meaning of the text?
- How is my understanding of my own identity transformed through reading the text?

Youth literacies and identities are also socially constructed (Moje & Luke, 2009). In other words, when students interact with their peers in spaces such as book clubs, their textual interpretations and understanding of the self can all be renegotiated through their engagements, through what they learn from others and how they connect with them. And remember from culturally sustaining pedagogies that these literacies and identities are fluid and interactive, prone to changes, contradictions, and permeable readings and identity constructions.

Before looking at specific strategies for infusing emotional and identity-based work, it's important that we first briefly explore and understand reader response theories and how they intersect with culturally sustaining pedagogies. Coined by Louise Rosenblatt, reader response theory is grounded in the notion of "transaction," where the reader and text come together to make meaning (Rosenblatt, 1994).

Remember that graphic from Chapter 1 (see Figure 1.1)? The figure below offers a reminder of that transactional process, where the text and self intersect, promoting a process for students' literacy and emotional development.

Reader response theory shifts traditional textual interactions of one solitary meaning to multiple reader interpretations that are constructed through a prism of students' beliefs, cultural backgrounds, value systems, and lived experiences.

During these transactions, readers can engage in two different processes, termed *efferent* and *aesthetic*. During the efferent process, readers work to acquire new information, whereas the aesthetic process is unique because meaning construction is different based on readers' experiences. Rosenblatt (1994) argued that these aesthetic transactions enhance readers' emotional capacities, increasing cognitive and affective development. Extending Rosenblatt's theories, Probst (2004) explained that these aesthetic transactions are a critical part of youth identity development. We must also keep in mind that reader response theory is culturally situated (Brooks & Browne, 2012), where youth textual interpretations are influenced by their cultural and linguistic backgrounds, their various abilities, and their lived experiences.

So how does all of this fit within book clubs? First, there is no one way to interpret a text. Reader response theory enacts culturally sustaining approaches in that we should allow students to bring their complex identities to the circle, to make meaning of the text and discuss how it fits within their worlds. It also means that interpretations are fluid. For example, students may come to book club with one understanding and then leave with a different one after engaging with their peers. As facilitators, we must then be open to multiple interpretations and ways of being, as students will bring their diversities to the reading and discussions. In allowing for that freedom, we give students agency to interpret the text in ways that connect to their own emotional well-being and identity construction.

As facilitators, we can directly support our students' reading development and emotional literacies by combining critical reading strategies with identity and emotional-based layering. We will look at eight reading strategies that we can teach and model through the explicit instruction discussed above. The following strategies are research based and will aid in our students' comprehension of the text (the efferent process of transactional reading) while also centering their identities and emotional literacies (the aesthetic process of transactional reading). I will use examples from the book *Written in the Stars* (Saeed, 2016), which a group of my students read during the pandemic. As all of the young men were in their mid- to late teens, and all of Muslim descent from various Middle Eastern and African countries, they wanted to read a text that centered the life of a person experiencing an arranged marriage. The counselor and I offered them several options, and they unanimously selected *Written in the Stars*, as they were curious to read and learn from the perspective of an adolescent female. In this story, the main character, Naila, has a secret relationship with Saif. When her parents find out, they take her to Pakistan, their home country, to find her a husband. The following eight reading strategies will highlight how we focused on reading comprehension while integrating emotional and identity-based work.

IMPORTANT NOTE TO FACILITATORS

As facilitators, we often may not share the same identities and communities as our students in book club. Our students may select texts that do not intersect with our own identities and lived experiences. As a white woman, not of Muslim descent and born in the United States, I found many aspects of my identity were clearly different from the young men in this book club. However, arranged marriages was a topic they wanted to explore, because the issue was important to them. Many of the young men were separated from their families, living with cousins, aunts, and uncles, while their parents stayed behind for financial reasons. Therefore, many expressed their mixed feelings about missing out on the opportunity to have their marriages arranged in their home countries. As a facilitator, I listened to the emotional needs of my students and offered them texts that matched their interests. My role was certainly not to judge students' perspectives or positionalities. I learned so much from the text and from the young men. And sometimes I did not agree with them. Some spoke to limiting the freedoms of the young women in their lives, while others spoke back to those perspectives. In doing so, we engaged in tough conversations about women's rights and religious traditions.

While we often did not agree on issues, we did establish a safe space where the young men listened and engaged with one another in ways that valued each other's perspectives and experiences. During one conversation, for example, we talked about the differences between arranged and forced marriages. Idris said he thought it was his right, as a future father, to marry his daughters to whom he felt best, regardless of their aspirations. Zeke immediately replied, "I want my daughter to be a doctor *first* and then she can get married." Often the young men asked us what we thought. Asaf, in particular, would often say, "I want to ask Ms. Jody what she thinks." And I was honest with them.

Because of my positionality, I encouraged the young men to bring questions and topics to our book club sessions. Ultimately, the questions and the topics *should* always come from our students, as we want them to become independent thinkers, readers, and communicators. Yet, our identities may get in the way of that. I understand that if I were a man, or Muslim, or an immigrant, the students may have engaged with me in very different ways. We must explicitly acknowledge those differences in our spaces and be vulnerable to what we do and do not understand.

In looking at the reading strategies below, I will offer examples of types of questions we can ask to develop our students' reading skills and emotional literacies. As facilitators, regardless of our identities, we must prioritize students' inquiries first and foremost, yet also be prepared with questions and tools to challenge and push students' thinking while simultaneously considering how we can help them to become more critical readers.

1. **Activating Prior Knowledge:** Students will better understand and connect to texts if they think about what they already know and have experienced, considering how that intersects with the context of the reading (Lee & Spratley, 2010). Thus, we might ask before beginning *Written in the Stars*, "What are your thoughts on arranged marriages? What have been your experiences within your families? Is this tradition an important part of your identity and community?" When asking these questions, we are activating prior knowledge and thinking about our identities as they connect with the characters' experiences. Before reading *Written in the Stars*, my students discussed their own families; for some of them, marriages were still arranged for them or for their immediate family members. The young men then discussed whether they agreed or disagreed with these traditions, allowing us to get to know each other and sparking interest before reading the book.

2. **Summarizing:** Making summaries, both individually and collectively within book clubs, can be a critical strategy in that it increases students' comprehension and provides a foundation and gateway for deeper interpretation and analysis (Carnine, Silbert, Kame'enui, & Tarver, 2010; Graham & Hebert, 2010). Summaries can serve multiple purposes. Sometimes, we will find that students have not done the reading—and that is okay. We should then use the rich human resources in our book club and have them summarize the text for others. When this has happened, those summaries often inspire readers who are somewhat hesitant or reluctant to read. Sometimes, readers use summaries as springboards for more in-depth analysis. For example, we asked the youth in the *Written in the Stars* book club, "Summarize how the parents reacted when they found out about Naila's secret relationship. How does she feel? How did her parents feel?" This line of questioning allows for reading comprehension and integration of emotional discussions. In this case, collectively, the young men summarized the characters' reactions, which seamlessly led to a conversation about how they felt about the parents' responses. After listening to the summary, Asaf said, "It makes sense they are angry. They think they have failed as parents. They are embarrassed. It's not good. The father is angry, but they should talk and eat together." Zeke agreed, adding, "I don't think they should worry about what their friends and other people think about them." In this scenario, students use the summary to talk about the characters' complex emotions, while establishing strategies to communicate with families in collaborative ways.

3. **Making Connections:** Making connections is the pathway to deeper interpretations. Reading researchers argue that making connections gets students motivated to read and engage in stronger analysis

(Lenski, Wham, Johns, & Caskey, 2007). In my 20 years of facilitating book clubs, this is the strategy that students lean to the most because it allows them to thoughtfully integrate their identities and lived experiences as they connect to the texts. Personal connection also helps students develop their lifelong love of reading—where they begin to see themselves and their communities within the texts. We might ask students to engage in different types of connections, such as text-to-self, text-to-world, and text-to-text, explaining what these connections are and modeling what they look like.

During one book club session for *Written in the Stars*, we asked, "What does Naila see for herself in the future? What does she want to do with her life? How about you? What decisions have you made about your future—and what do you see for yourself?" This line of questioning begins with the springboard of discussing the main character but then allows students to talk about making informed decisions. Articulating our futures and sharing those dreams with others is a powerful way to help students set goals that are grounded in their interests and passions. On the website are other sample mini-lessons for making connections.

4. **Monitoring Our Reading:** Teaching students to monitor their comprehension, or engage in what is called *metacognition*, can be very difficult, but when we do think about our reading as we read, we can gain deeper understanding of the text and begin to use corrective strategies when needed (Boardman et al., 2008). During book club, we might read passages together and then model what this process looks and sounds like so that students can try it out with other chapters on their own. We can explicitly ask questions such as, "When you read this week, think about your thinking as you are reading. This is metacognition! What kinds of things go on in your mind as you read? Jot those down on a piece of paper or into your phone. You might think about how you are seeing your identities and lived experiences. How might Naila and her family remind you of your own communities?" These questions again get at both the metacognitive strategy of monitoring our reading and provides students with a focus where they can think about their own identities and how they connect to the characters.

5. **Asking Questions:** Asking questions is a strategy we want students to develop both to help them understand the text and as a way to enhance our book club conversations. Asking questions also helps activate students' prior knowledge, engage in clarifications of interpretations, and inspire reading motivation (Boardman et al., 2008). Research suggests that writing questions and answering those inquiries helps make information from the text easier for students to retain while also providing them with more opportunities to interact

with the content (Graham & Hebert, 2010). We might give students a mini-lesson followed by modeling where we explain different types of questions while also offering students examples of what those questions can look like (see the website for an example). To infuse emotional literacies, we can also provide students with targeted questioning such as, "As you read this week, think about questions you want to ask each other for our next book club. Perhaps focus on Naila's emotions while she is in Pakistan. How is she feeling? Why is she feeling that way?" In this way, students are still offered choice in making their own questions and afforded opportunities to engage with the main character's emotions.

6. **Making Inferences:** Making inferences and developing analysis are the most challenging reading skills but the ones that are the most prevalent in our standardized tests. Making inferences is a foundational skill that leads students to deeper analysis (Marzano, 2010). To make those inferences, readers need to think about and refer to textual evidence and combine that with their own background knowledge to gain deeper meanings and interpretations. Making inferences also requires that students make connections between ideas, characters, and events while also cognitively filling in information that may not be explicitly stated. When readers make these inferences, they deepen their comprehension and are better able to engage in complex conversations with their peers. On the website is a graphic organizer that may assist your students with making inferences. As an example, for our line of questioning, we can combine inferring with making informed decisions, asking students, "Naila's family decides she will never return to the U.S. Based on what you've read so far, why do you think they've made that decision? Do you agree or disagree with that decision? Tell us why. How might you feel if the same decision was made for you or someone in your family?"

7. **Analyzing the Text:** When students can successfully make inferences, they are on the path to deep analysis. Analysis is a rich interpretation, where students look at the text holistically, rather than focusing on the smaller passages (Thompson, 2018). Analysis asks students to look at the relationships between events, ideas, and characters—recognizing and interpreting patterns and themes—and then drawing conclusions about the text. We might demonstrate this skill visually to students as the following:

The idea here is to ask students to think about the evidence they've discussed thus far, to engage in analysis, thinking about the text as a whole, the author's purpose, the themes of the book, and critical representations the text may be making about our communities. For example, we might ask, "How does Naila's identity change over time?" In this way, we are asking readers to analyze the text holistically, looking for those themes and patterns as they connect to Naila; at the same time, we are asking them to explore issues of identity, specifically how our identities—our ways of being—change and are fluid. In our book club, after discussing this question, we asked the young men, "We've talked about Naila's development. How do you think you've changed since moving to the U.S.?" Notice that we begin with the safety net of analyzing Naila's character but then use her experiences as a springboard for the young men to articulate and share their own sense of growth over time.

8. **Evaluating the Text:** A final reading strategy we want to develop in readers is their ability to evaluate texts, offering their assessments about how the plots unfold and how the characters develop, as well as the overall quality of the writing. This strategy allows students to form opinions of various texts based on textual evidence and their own reading preferences. Thus, we might ask, "What did you think about the book overall? Do you think the author's portrayal of the situations—of the identities presented—was realistic? Talk to us about why or why not." Again, we are asking students to engage in a critical reading strategy—assessing and evaluating texts—while also thinking about how identities are positioned and presented by the authors, thus encompassing both reading and emotional development for students.

On the website, you will find a chart that offers an overview of these eight reading strategies, providing sample questions from *Written in the Stars*. These strategies have been aligned with the three different ways we can fold in emotional and identity-based engagements (i.e., cultivating self-awareness and identity development, developing emotional literacies and self-care, and engaging in informed decision making). Note that many of these reading strategies also overlap with Common Core and Next Gen standards that address reading competencies.

HOW DO WE INTEGRATE WRITING INTO BOOK CLUBS?

Earlier in this chapter, I talked about literacy being more than just reading, that it entails our abilities to write and communicate as well. While this book focuses primarily on reading and discussions, we can also integrate meaningful writing opportunities into our book clubs. Developing students' writing is incredibly important as strong writing skills are predictors for students' overall academic success and are critical aspects for participation in civic democracies (Graham & Perin, 2007). Writing also has emotional benefits in that youth can express their emotions, engaging in healing practices that positively impact their well-being (Goodwin & Jones, 2020; Pennebaker & Smyth, 2016). Tatum (2013) found that culturally relevant and justice-based writing experiences allowed youth to develop their sense of identity, helping nurture resilience and intellectual growth. He explains, "To write is to become familiar with your light and darkness and everything in between. It becomes the gray matter of your existence. Reading puts you in contact with others. Writing puts you in contact with yourself" (p. 3). Further, writing provides spaces for students to confront oppression they may be experiencing based on their intersectional identities (Johnson, 2017; Johnson & Eubanks, 2015).

What do we know about research in writing instruction? First, students need to write—and they need to write a lot. They also need choice, and they need to write for authentic purposes and for authentic audiences. When including writing in our book clubs, we must ensure that we are doing so in culturally sustaining ways, where we help students connect their writing to the texts they are reading, most importantly to their identities, lived experiences, and larger communities (Johnson & Eubanks, 2015; Winn & Johnson, 2011). In this book, we've already discussed many ways to infuse writing into book clubs. How much and when depends on the purpose of your book club, the students who are participating, and the context. Are you a classroom teacher who wants to connect reading to writing? Or, are you a counselor or social worker who wants to use both reading *and* writing for therapeutic purposes?

Will you do informal writing to complement the reading and assess students' comprehension? If so, recall Chapter 4. Those assessments are examples of writing integration, from writing out their role sheets to responding on sticky notes or in their graphic organizers and bookmarks. Journaling—either individually, with the facilitator, or with a peer—can also be a wonderful way to process the content of the book while also discussing critical issues around students' identities and emotional literacies as they connect to the characters. As an example, students could keep gratitude journals to express what they are grateful for in life. Perhaps they can also write about the characters in the books and share what they think the characters can be grateful for. In this way, we are not just focusing on the trauma that the characters and students may be experiencing, but also centering joy—and what gives us space to dream and imagine.

Students can engage in other informal writing experiences, either as an opening or a closing ritual to your book club sessions. Maybe students could write a letter to one of the characters, a peer, or even themselves. We can ask students questions based on the eight reading strategies explained previously to assess their reading, while also offering authentic writing experiences and spaces for emotional literacy development. Students who want to partake in more creative exercises can use poetry or mind mapping, where they combine images and writing to express their emotions as they connect to the texts.

Technology is also a great resource. Students can use Google Docs, develop a blog, or send tweets. The point here is to offer students choice in how they engage in the writing process. For those students who might be emergent writers or bi- and multilingual learners, we might offer them the following sample sentence starters to help them craft some of their responses:

- I connected to the character _____, when . . .
- The character _____ reminds me of . . .
- The character felt sad/angry/frustrated when . . .
- An important decision the character made was . . .

We can also use more extensive summative writing assessments that connect to the texts we read. Returning to Chapter 4, students could create Facebook or yearbook representations of the texts, they could write readers theater scripts, or they could write poetry or songs that are inspired by the content in the books. Our writing assignments might also be justice-oriented, where students use their writing—their voices—to advocate for themselves and others.

The options are limitless when it comes to how we want to use writing in the book club process—and, again, our choices should always depend on our students' needs. For now, let's pause and use our template to think about the context of your book clubs. What reading strategies and writing opportunities might you infuse that address our focus on emotional and identity-based work?

Infusing Literacy Strategies Into Emotional and Identity-Based Work	
What reading strategies might you infuse into your book club/s? How will these align with your attention to emotional and identity-based work?	What writing opportunities might you offer students? How will these align with emotional and identity-based work?

QR Code for Chapter 5 Resources

CHAPTER 6

Developing Students' Social Awareness, Interpersonal Relationships, and Agency

It is nearly 3 years to the day since Betsy and Fay so courageously shared with our book club the pain associated with the loss of their mothers. The young women are now all seniors, and this is our fourth year together, still meeting on Thursdays after school, in the same conference room, eating the same cheese slices from the local pizzeria. Our first meeting of the year begins in a flurry: Tia shares her prom dress ideas, Joy speaks about an internship she has started at a fashion magazine, and Mary—our newest member—tells us about an anime series she is binge-watching. We talk about our summers. I ask the young women about their college applications and their new teachers, and we easily slide back into the comfort of book club.

Once we've caught up, I make a proposition: "Book club has been terrific. Clearly. My most favorite part of the week. I am beyond grateful for this experience. We've read everything under the sun, talking about love, peers, families. I was thinking that this year, perhaps we could have a different focus—one where we employ more critical lenses, where we might step away a bit from young adult—and try out more adult contemporary texts that reflect our greater world and communities—ones that speak intentionally to injustices various populations have been grappling with historically, currently, locally, globally. Whaddaya think?"

Sofia responds skeptically, "Well, that sounds great—as long as it doesn't get boring—and we can still talk about our lives."

"Yes, of course!" I say, trying to alleviate her concerns. "Book club will always center your lives, and I promise you, the texts and conversations will not get boring, as you still have control over our content. You all are going away to college soon so I thought we might try reading some books that might reflect what you'll be reading in the future. You still get choice over our books, of course, but let's maybe think about trying something new and challenging, something rewarding to get us out of our high school bubble. Does that make sense?"

"I love it!" shouts Fay, tapping her fingers eagerly on our table. "We're all going to college next year. We can't just read about high school drama anymore. It's time we really think about what's going on."

"Agreed!" Mary exclaims. "What should we read?"

We make arrangements for a Saturday meet-up at a local bookstore near our school. Usually we gravitate to the young adult section—but today we venture into the adult fiction area, taking over the narrow aisle and picking up books that look interesting. The transition to contemporary literature was a deliberate choice on my part, as I felt after 3 years of working together and in preparation for college, the young women were ready to grapple with novels that they might experience in the future. As facilitators, we want to always hold high expectations while allowing for choice, but we also want to challenge our students and expose them to texts and ideas they may not have considered previously. Of course, this decision was collaborative, where I brought up the idea but the young women ultimately made the textual selections and during book clubs chose the topics and questions that we discussed.

That year, the young women read a variety of texts, from Audre Lorde's (1982) biomythography, *Zami: A New Spelling of My Name,* to Arundhati Roy's (2008) *The God of Small Things.* We talked about racism and colorism, heteronormativity and gender norms, and caste systems and socioeconomic inequities. Despite this new focus, I still continually checked in with the young women to ensure that their concerns were addressed and that book club still served as a space to center their interests and passions.

That year, the young women continued to make powerful connections from the texts to their lives, often speaking to their experiences with racism, sexism, and homophobia. We talked about who had power and why in the texts, and in the same breath, we discussed who maintains power in the United States and the world and why. Our conversations were both localized and global. The young women spoke to their intersectionalities: what it was like as Latinas, as bilingual women of color, as children of immigrants who experience stereotyping, marginalization, and discrimination. Mary, for example, often talked about her Chinese family, while Fay shared aspects of her African heritage and how racism and sexism proliferated differently as she straddled her father's Kenyan culture along with her U.S. experiences. The young women also spoke of internalized racism and colorism, discussing the historical roots of slavery and colonialism and their impact on our current systems and ways of being.

Most importantly, the young women used book club to build their sense of agency. They talked about the writers' and characters' acts of resistance—and how they could emulate those actions in their own lives. They discussed strategies for advocating for themselves and for others and strategies for participating in social justice work.

At the end of the year, I took the young women out to lunch to celebrate our time together. We used this moment to laugh and reminisce and reflect on what we gained from this new focus. Sofia and Mary said they found the book club empowering. Mary explained, "It was a time I could release my energy and just talk and not be worried about being judged."

"Yes!" agreed Tia enthusiastically. "It felt like family. We talked about race, class, and gender, but if we had a problem, we could talk about it. We still had that space."

Sofia nodded her head and said, "The book club lets us release feelings of oppression. You feel something within yourself, and you wanna—no, you need to—get it out. Even though you may disagree, you might change someone's perspective. We were comfortable and confided in each other."

"Exactly," Joy added. "Book club opened me up and helped me because like Tia or Sofia would talk about things. Now I've thought about them, especially with all the stuff I've been going through with my family. They taught *me* to open up. We had that time together and formed friendships."

I met with these young women again after their first year of college, and during that time, it was like we had never been apart. The young women talked about how the final year of book club influenced how they viewed their worlds and how they engaged within their new communities. Mary had read every book by Anchee Min to connect with her Chinese heritage. Sofia had joined the Latino Student Organization, while Fay had started using the African name her mother had given her and was learning Swahili. The women attributed these changes to the influences they had on one another.

This chapter will speak directly to how we can create these kinds of spaces for our students. We will delve into how book clubs can be used to develop students' speaking and listening literacies while also helping to enhance their social awareness, relationships with others, and sense of agency.

HOW CAN WE USE BOOK CLUBS TO DEVELOP STUDENTS' SOCIAL LITERACIES?

Engaging socially with others in classrooms or communities can be arduous for adolescents and adults alike. Trying to figure out the right time to say something, trying not to be worried about what we've said, and trying to negotiate how to speak back to someone without shutting them down are just a few of the struggles that many of us encounter when participating in groups.

A critical part of adolescent social development is helping youth build their conversational dispositions and speaking and listening literacies. In doing this work, we must remember that we have students from a range of cultural backgrounds, where their ways of interacting may not mirror what we are accustomed to. Thus, we must consider the following:

- In our personal and professional lives, how do we engage in speaking and listening with others? How do our families and communities do so?

- What ways are our interactions the same as and different from those of our students? How can we work to not impose our cultural ways of engaging on them?

I think back to my own family on my father's side, who have Italian roots and were born and raised in the bustling streets of Brooklyn. Some outsiders (my Floridian mother to be sure) thought my family was loud, that we gestured too much with our hands, and that we interrupted each other. Yet perhaps for others, this way of engaging feels and sounds very familiar and comfortable.

These cultural experiences translated to many of my teaching practices. I never minded a loud classroom; I love it when students get excited or charged about a topic or text. Not all of us may have that instructional approach—and that's okay. Students need to experience different kinds of classrooms and communities so that when they are adults, they can adjust to various ways of engagement in college or career. That being said, our primary objective must always be about creating inclusive spaces that acknowledge, honor, and incorporate the diversities our students bring.

We must remember not to silence, marginalize, nor reprimand students for cultural ways of being that may be different from our own. We also cannot be color-blind, expecting "norms" for classroom or small-group behaviors. DiAngelo (2018) warns us that "while the idea of color blindness may have started as a well-intentioned strategy for interrupting racism, in practice it served to deny the reality of racism and thus hold it in place" (p. 42). Within systems of education, Hall, Johnson, Juzwik, Wortham, and Mosley (2010) found that teachers with color-blind attitudes do not understand or dismantle ways in which they privilege particular literacy practices—often those of white, middle-class engagements and discourses. In ignoring cultural, linguistic, and neurological differences, facilitators will marginalize and silence students in group settings.

One way to be mindful of this marginalization is through continual self-reflection and feedback from students. At the end of the week, for example, I provide my students with exit tickets, asking them about how they are feeling within our community:

- Describe a time you felt joy or pride this week.
- Describe a time when you felt disappointed or frustrated.
- Is there any way I can help you feel more included and heard in the classroom or in book club?

These questions allow me to receive continual feedback about how I interact with students and give me suggestions for modifying my instruction and facilitation to better meet student needs and be more inclusive.

Another method is to co-construct agreements for book clubs, which we talked about in Chapter 4. Having explicit conversations and shared decision making about how we interact with one another is critical. These agreements do not have to be static all year. In my own experiences as a facilitator, we kept those agreements on chart paper visible throughout our time together, and we changed them when an issue came up that we felt justified a revised or additional agreement.

Finally, as facilitators, we can provide mini-lessons about how to participate in small groups. Think back to Chapter 4, where I discussed offering students mini-lessons to help build their discussion skills. Specifically, I spoke about a lesson on listening and responding without judgment. I also talked about mini-lessons on asking questions that lead to substantial conversations. These are powerful methods that respond to the differentiated supports our students may need.

Regarding social development, let's look first at the practice of listening, a skill that is often overlooked in our classrooms yet is vital for us to understand and connect. As facilitators, listening is a skill we want to discuss explicitly with students, explaining first and foremost that "listening is not a passive act" (Dobson, 2012, p. 853) but something we want to improve continually.

With every book club, I have conversations about what it means to be a listener. Why is listening so important? What is our goal in listening to each other? My students and I talk about the primary goal of listening: understanding and connecting. As listeners, we can engage in four different activities: We can visualize, summarize, connect, and be reflective of how we are responding emotionally to what we hear (Alford, 2020). To model these processes, we might watch a YouTube clip or invite a community member into our space and ask students to participate actively as they listen: What are they seeing? What are they hearing? How are they connecting? What are they feeling? Perhaps after listening, have students jot down those thoughts (their summaries, visualizations, connections, and feelings) and then share them with a partner or small group. That fourth aspect of listening, reflecting on our emotions, is critically important to establish and maintain safety within our group settings. I often ask my students to dig deep into those feelings: What kinds of emotions arise as you listen? How do these emotions make you want to respond? We then talk about what we can do if we have strong emotional responses. Schieble, Vetter, and Martin (2020) offer the following prompt for youth: "Right now, I find myself having an emotional reaction to what you said. To make sure that I understand what you mean, let me summarize what I heard" (p. 61). This sample response acknowledges that we have emotions, and instead of ignoring them or reacting immediately, we can articulate those feelings openly and then ask for clarification.

My students and I also speak about the importance of not interrupting. Since our goal is to understand and connect, we want to make sure we hear the speaker's perspective before jumping in with our thoughts. I suggest that students monitor their attention: Are you thinking about what the speaker is saying—or are you thinking about what you want to say next? These are important reflections to incorporate when building students' active listening skills. For students who struggle with this skill, I might suggest taking notes or doodling. While writing or sketching might seem like "bad" listening behavior, the visuals and the kinesthetics of doing so may help some youth better track what is said.

The following list offers other suggestions for teaching active listening skills:

- Model active listening every day. When students share, be quiet, make eye contact, nod your head, and ask follow-up questions. Then stop and think aloud with students: "What did I do that showed Amira I was listening to her?"
- After observing book clubs, provide students with feedback about what you notice about their listening. Do you see eye contact? Are we nodding our heads as we listen? Are we responding directly to what the person is talking about?
- Provide time for students to practice active listening, especially if you notice students struggling. Brief reminder exercises help students to return to more active stances as listeners. On the website, you will find examples of other critical listening exercises.
- Talk to students about wait time. Longer pauses are okay, despite the discomfort, and give others time to think before responding. You might tell students to purposefully practice wait time as they ask each other questions.
- Provide students with sentence starters that demonstrate to others we've heard what they said before moving on to our own ideas. Here are some examples:

  "I really liked what you said about _____"
  "What you said about_____ reminded me of _____"
  "I wonder what you mean when you said _____"
  "While I agree with what you said, I think _____"

- Talk to students about listening as an act of love. When we listen to each other, we show that we care and want to know one another. In book clubs, conversations can get emotional, so we want students to build skills for responding to what they've heard. I use Hill's language (2009) in calling these efforts "co-signing," where students affirm each other, especially when they are vulnerable. One way to engage in co-signing is through encouraging the speaker to continue (e.g., using nonverbal or body language, interjecting with encouraging words, or offering complementary narratives). A second way is to validate a speaker's truths by agreeing or connecting to what they said.

Like the development of listening, we also want to help students with their speaking skills. This can be challenging for quieter or shyer students, students with speech impediments, or students who are new to the language spoken in book clubs. One way to help alleviate students' trepidation is to begin small. As a classroom teacher, for example, I seat my students in pairs so that they have many opportunities to practice turning and talking with their partners and building relationships. Those partnerships change throughout the year, based on student dynamics and feedback about their seating, but the idea is to get them comfortable talking often with others. And by often, I mean every day.

It is also critical that we be mindful of our language positionalities, again reflecting on how we may impose our own ways of speaking onto students. We do not want to shut students down by continually correcting their forms of communication; in doing so, we decrease their motivations for speaking in that they may become more concerned about talking "correctly" and making mistakes, rather than offering their opinions, ideas, and emotions (Metz, 2020). Often facilitators privilege dominant and white mainstream English, participating in linguistic racism and white linguistic supremacy (Alim & Smitherman, 2012; Baker-Bell, 2020; Paris, 2009), which creates linguistic and racial hierarchies that diminish the safety of our communities.

To support our linguistically, neurologically, and culturally diverse students, we must then reflect on our own biases and center the quality of our students' ideas, rather than focusing on their linguistic ways of being (Kirkland, 2010). While it is helpful for students to access academic and mainstream Englishes, we must acknowledge to ourselves and with our students that discourse patterns are rooted in historical systems of discrimination (Alim, 2005; Metz, 2020). Explicit conversations like these with youth open up important discussions of linguistic hierarchies that may encourage students to use their languages of comfort (Metz, 2020)—those that will best represent who they are and how they engage with the texts.

With these guiding tenets in mind, we can still provide students with specific mini-lessons grounded in their needs that will help them to develop as speakers. Offering mini-lessons is an impactful way to move students to become more intentional participants. We might, for example, create chart paper signage that offers speakers the following suggestions:

- Use textual evidence to support your ideas.
- Ask questions that engage others.
- Build on each other's ideas; refer to what others have said and make connections between your ideas and theirs.
- Critique ideas in ways that won't shut others down but will help them to see different perspectives.
- Participate, but also monitor how much you talk, thinking about ways to invite others in.
- Praise and lift each other up.

Each of these suggestions can be broken down into individual mini-lessons. The more targeted instructional lessons we provide—that offer modeling and sentence starters—the better we can support students.

Finally, it is of utmost importance that we are vigilant when it comes to monitoring how different students participate in book clubs. Lewis and Zisselsberger (2018), for example, did an intensive study of middle school book clubs, where they found that while the facilitators *intended* the spaces to offer more opportunities for emergent bilingual students to speak, instead their contributions were not honored, which ultimately led to their withdrawal from discussions. Similarly, Evans (1996) found that when students were in mixed-gendered groups, male students tended to tease—and even threaten—female students. As facilitators, then, we must have a strong sense of what is happening in our book clubs, offering guidance so as to avoid marginalization of students. If we see youth behaviors that are silencing of others or if we find students are withdrawing from book clubs, we can vary our supports based on student need. Perhaps we offer whole-group mini-lessons or reconfigure our groups. We can also provide individualized feedback to students to help them participate in more inclusive and empathetic ways.

Remember that our ultimate goals for book clubs are inclusion and transformation. If we are not protective of the safety of these spaces, then we can damage and harm young people. We want to be aware of silencing or bullying and immediately intervene and support students as they work to develop their linguistic dispositions and their speaking and listening literacies. And while we never want to position ourselves as the center of book clubs, because they should be student-led, our role in monitoring with follow-up support is paramount to ensure equity of voices.

As facilitators, we also want to thoughtfully honor the linguistic diversities that students bring. This means encouraging students to read books and have conversations in their home languages. When I work with multilingual book clubs, I always try to have at least two students who share the same linguistic heritage in one group so that if either of them experiences confusion based on the primary language spoken, they have a partner to rely on. I understand, however, that this may not always be possible if there is only one student who speaks a particular language; in this case, I recommend pairing this student with another student who has strong skills in empathy and patience, who can help support those who might feel insecure or uncomfortable.

Our students come to us with incredible skills in languages and dispositions for relationships. Let's build on those assets then and use them to create safe, inclusive spaces. For now, let's turn to our template to think about ways we can help students develop those necessary literacy skills for safe, courageous, and empowering conversations.

Supporting Students' Speaking and Listening Literacies	
What are your students' strengths and assets when thinking about their speaking and listening literacies?	
What are areas where students can use support when developing their active listening skills?	What are areas where students can use support when thinking about their conversation skills?

HOW CAN BOOK CLUBS CENTER SOCIAL AWARENESS?

In the previous chapter, I talked about how we can enhance students' literacies in reading and writing while also attending to their emotional and identity development. We are now going to layer onto that work: developing students' skills of speaking and listening (as discussed above) along with their social development, which includes building social awareness, developing relationships, and enhancing youth sense of agency. Figure 6.1 provides a synopsis of the social and emotional literacies we are discussing.

Let's explore the first area of social development, social awareness, which is a young person's ability to understand diverse perspectives and empathize with others, particularly those from backgrounds and cultures that may be different from their own (CASEL, 2020; Simmons, 2019). Social awareness includes honoring and respecting diversities and acting with compassion for others. It also includes raising critical consciousness in that social awareness encourages students to unpack historical and current injustices, asking youth to "recognize how their individual experiences are tethered to larger systems" (Strong & McMain, 2020, p. 6).

The first aspect of social awareness is exposing students to various perspectives so that they can begin to understand, honor, and respect diverse

Figure 6.1. Emotional and Social Development

Emotional Development (Chapter 5)	Social Development (Chapter 6)
Cultivating self-awareness and identity development	Building social awareness
Developing emotional literacies and self-care	Developing relationships
Engaging in informed decision making	Enhancing students' sense of agency

cultures, languages, and abilities. Book clubs are an important opportunity to develop these understandings. For example, to help students understand the lived experiences of Indigenous populations, there are many young adult titles by Native authors to help non-Native youth enhance their knowledge of Indigenous histories, cultures, beliefs, rituals, and languages. Sample texts written by and about Indigenous peoples are offered on the website. Similarly, we might ask able-bodied or neurotypical students to read texts about various physical challenges and neurodiversities (sample texts are on the website).

Using texts as "windows" (Bishop, 1990), we can invite students to better understand and respect diversities. We can also use these textual worlds to incorporate the development of students' empathy, a powerful disposition that allows for healing-centered engagements. Empathy allows us to connect and understand others' experiences and emotions. When we help students develop empathy, they may be less apt to get angry at someone or to shut someone out during book clubs, because we are working toward connecting to each other.

In book clubs, students can participate in two different types of empathy in which we can speak to them directly:

1. **Cognitive empathy** is our ability to take on perspectives, to imagine what it is like to live in another person's shoes, and to understand someone else's feelings.
2. **Affective empathy** is when we begin to feel or share the emotions of others.

In reading *Firekeeper's Daughter* (Boulley, 2021), for example, the main character, Daunis, a biracial, unenrolled tribal member of the Ojibwe peoples, struggles between the cultures of her white family (the Fontaines) and that of her Indigenous family (the Firekeepers). Boulley writes, "I learned there were times when I was expected to be a Fontaine and other times when it was safe to be a Firekeeper" (p. 11). Questions we might pose to students in this book club include, "What do you think it is like for Daunis to live in two different worlds? How do you think this existence feels? How does Daunis learn to bridge both worlds, cultures, and languages?" These questions allow for cognitive empathy, where students are encouraged to unpack Daunis's perspectives to better understand her experiences.

Questions that might evoke students' sense of affective empathy might be, "Have you ever felt like you lived in two different worlds? How so? How did this make you feel?" We can begin with the cognitive empathy questions first, as these allow safety in discussing the characters' experiences; however, affective empathy questions lead to students' connections to the text and the characters' emotions. We never want to force students to reveal these feelings, but we do want to offer that door to encourage them to share their stories and take emotional risks by being vulnerable, open, and honest (Ginwright, 2018). Anzaldua (2002) explains that through the telling of painful experiences, we can "transform them into something valuable, *algo para compartir* or share with others so they too may be empowered" (p. 540).

Empathy-building can also lead to consciousness-raising. For marginalized students, this work is critical in that they can share their similarities to characters and each other around such issues as oppression and discrimination. Building social awareness and encouraging courageous conversations allow vulnerable students to address the larger sociopolitical contexts in which they live and discuss how inequities impact their lives so that they can collectively build strategies for justice (Simmons, 2019).

This work is also important for white students who need to develop their understanding of diversities, while also acknowledging their own privilege to consider ways they can leverage that power to dismantle oppressive systems. Bishop (1990) reminds us that youth from dominant social groups suffer when they are not exposed to diverse experiences; they need those windows into reality so that they can appreciate and honor our multicultural and multilingual worlds. The same is true for other types of consciousness-raising, from having our neurotypical and able-bodied students read books about diverse abilities to having our monolingual students read books about youth who experience linguistic racism and marginalization. Through targeted questions, intentional book choices, and scaffolding, we can use book clubs to build students' social awareness, which not only develops their skills in reading, speaking, and listening, but—most importantly—enhances their dispositions to create a kinder and more just world.

HOW CAN BOOK CLUBS HELP STUDENTS DEVELOP RELATIONSHIPS?

Overwhelmingly, every year, when I get feedback on book clubs, youth are grateful for how these spaces help them not only talk about their personal relationships but, more importantly, develop relationships with each other. Gina talked about this phenomenon with her book group: "We all hang. Now I see other book club members in the hall, and I'm like, 'Hey, you read the book?' I mean, I used to say 'hi' to them and we were in classes together but it was never like now. Me and Yoana got closer. Keisha, me, Eileen, and Carla have been close since forever but those other girls? Now we all hang out. It's cool. I loved my group."

Sofia had similar sentiments, sharing, "We all became friends. We would see each other on Thursdays or in the hallways or say 'hi,' or like Joy, I take the train with her now . . . you know the thing that connects us is the books . . . the books brought us together and we got to talk about our own experiences."

Creating and sustaining healthy and supportive relationships with diverse individuals and groups is a critical part of enhancing students' social development (CASEL, 2020; Simmons, 2019). To build relationships, youth need to communicate, listen actively, work collectively, and negotiate conflict constructively (Simmons, 2019). Building relationships with diverse individuals also means we need to lean into those social awareness skills described above—specifically having empathy and appreciation for diversities—while also standing up for our rights and the rights of others.

Establishing relationships is a huge part of adolescence (Poulin & Chan, 2010). While certainly relationship building is different for everyone—especially based on students' cultural and neurological backgrounds—research consistently points to the importance of relationships to adolescents' well-being (Bagwell & Schmidt, 2011). Having strong relationships means that we receive support, and it means we are part of communities that offer us intimacy. Developing relationships is also a critical socialization process that allows students to build their empathy, perspective-taking, and conflict-resolution skills, all important strategies to navigate our personal, professional, and academic worlds.

On the other hand, the absence of relationships with others can diminish youth well-being and is linked to negative mental health (Branje, van Aken, & van Lieshout, 2002; Kenny, Dooley, & Fitzgerald, 2014). When students engage and build relationships with others, they are less likely to feel lonely, experience depression, and have anxiety.

Further, transitioning from elementary to middle and high school can be challenging for youth. Often, students leave their small, intimate spaces of elementary school and enter larger and more impersonal secondary schools, where they may not know their peers (Veronneau & Dishion, 2011). Our relationships also change and evolve as we get older, especially as adolescents learn to adapt to new academic settings and grapple with conflicts in burgeoning relationships. Sometimes these challenges can become overwhelming, leading to stress, isolation, and declining academic achievement (Veronneau & Dishion, 2011).

During this time period, adolescents' relationships with their families also change (Kenny et al., 2014). Maintaining positive caregiver-adolescent connections is critical to sustain the well-being of youth (Kenny et al., 2014). This time period is also associated with youth discovering their gender and sexual identities while developing more sophisticated and nuanced romantic relationships (Furman, Low, & Ho, 2009).

It is a lot. But book clubs can be one way we help students collectively improve their connections with others.

In my experience, because relationships are so central to youth, most of our book club conversations centered these topics. My students, for example, often gravitated to discussions about how the characters navigated relationships with their families. Youth discussed both loving and controlling caregivers. They talked about everything from grandparents they adored to parents who were absent—and how these complicated relationships impacted the characters and themselves. Ultimately, if students felt safe and comfortable, book club became a place to speak to both the joys and traumas of families.

When Felicia talked about her own sexual abuse after reading about assault in *Speak* (Anderson, 1999), for instance, other young women in that book club supported her. They did not push her to elaborate but instead offered validation of her trauma, thanking her for her courage. This was a brave moment for Felicia but also a moment for empathy and relationship-building. Before our next meeting, I asked Felicia if we could debrief that moment together—without her having to share more. Relieved, Felicia responded, "Yes. I feel so weird about talking about it, and I'm wondering what the other girls thought."

For our next session, I opened up our conversations by asking, "How do we feel about last week's conversations about abuse? Why might these discussions be helpful as we work to lift each other up?"

Betsy shared first: "It was good we talked about those situations with family and what they did cause even though some girls may not have experienced it . . . it's something that girls should know in life so we know what to do and not just sit there and hide it."

Sofia agreed: "Yeah, even though it wasn't my experience, I wasn't afraid to talk about it. Felicia wasn't afraid, and it was those books that brought that out in us."

These opening comments started a flood of praise to and for Felicia—and Felicia then praised the others for their support. As a facilitator, I needed to merely unlock the door with a reflective question so that the young women could enter, gather, converse, and build each other up. In this way, we can see how youth use books and each other as support systems to cope with trauma and conflict in their families. Through these kinds of conversations— along with vulnerability, trust, and storytelling—young people also develop stronger relationships with each other.

Book clubs are also powerful places for youth to talk about their peer relationships. Since much of young adult literature focuses on the connections between adolescents, much of the conversation thus centers these issues. Depending on the books we read, students also have opportunities to talk about such struggles as bullying and harmful relationships, strategizing ways to stand up for themselves and others. While reading *Upstate* (Buckhanon, 2006), for example, one book club of all young women talked about how to advocate for equity in relationships. In this epistolary novel, the main character Antonio is convicted of a crime. While serving his sentence, Antonio and his girlfriend Natasha write letters back and forth. During one book club session, the young women spoke about Antonio's "controlling" language in one of his letters to Natasha.

Keisha heatedly shared: "Antonio said, 'I'll allow you to do what you want as long as something, something'? Some bullshit like that. I'm like get out of here. . . . 'I'll allow it.' I'm like, you'll allow it? How you going to allow me to do something? I'm my own person. I do what I want to do."

"Exactly," agreed Carla. "Nobody tells me what to do."

"It's like this," Keisha continued. "Me, you, me, you—if we're in a relationship, we have equal rights. I can't tell you to do nothing; you can't tell me to do nothing. . . . Why would I have to get permission from you to do something I want to do? To me, love is I trust you. Then everything else fades. I trust you. I love you."

A similar call for advocacy arose in another book club, while reading *Speak* (Anderson, 1999), where the main character is bullied by the "Marthas." These young women talked about how they had their own set of "Marthas" at our school, called the "BellaMafia," who often picked on other girls. They shared strategies for what they do when confronted by these young women and strategies for how they could defend others. Joy explained, "I just leave it alone, because I don't look for fights. But if they really start to target me then I have to. I wouldn't do stupid things like fight. . . . Fighting doesn't do anything. You just get a black eye. And then what? Nothing."

The other young women agreed, talking about ways to peacefully avoid confrontations, but we also talked about strategies for advocacy. Tia shared how she defended others who got picked on: "I normally curse people out for Gabrielle."

Fay said she did similar acts of advocacy, taking the time to reach out to Gabrielle to see if she's okay. She explained the advice she gave Gabrielle: "You can't let what they do stop you from being you."

For these book clubs, the conversations about peer relationships in the books became springboards for conversations about their own lives and how they navigate their authority and independence in relationships while also allowing for connections. The young women shared their stories and then offered advice about ways in which to build stronger relationships. Keisha later explained that these conversations were critical for her, sharing, "It helps to read about someone else's situations or to read about the person with the same situation and how they dealt with it."

Joy echoed Keisha's connection, offering, "The books were helpful 'cause I saw someone else doing what could have happened to me . . . and how they're acting it out, and I could say she did that wrong and I then could do this."

Let's take a moment to explore what this kind of work might look like in a classroom or small book club. At my previous school, as one example, I noticed the difficulties of new immigrants when they came into larger school spaces. One year, I had an especially shy student named Mei who recently moved from China. Speaking Mandarin fluently and having limited English, she kept to herself and rarely spoke. I checked in with her frequently, asking her questions about her interests, her transition, and her success in school. She always smiled when I approached, seeming both eager and nervous to talk.

"How is your book going?" I asked her one day.

"It is good," she replied.

"Have you talked to anyone about it yet?"

"Oh, no, miss. Never."

"What do you mean?"

"I don't talk to anyone at school, miss. Just you."

This last sentence caused me great alarm: How could we as a community who supported youth not notice this was happening? Frequently, our students who are new to English or new to the United States experience isolation—and because they can sometimes be quiet, teachers tend to focus on the more gregarious and outspoken students as our shyer students fade into our communities.

I intentionally seated Mei next to a young man who also spoke Mandarin, thinking they would connect. Research tells us that having same-ethnic friendships is important for developing positive ethnic identity (Graham, Munniksma, & Juvonen, 2013), yet her partner Zhang was also very shy—and so the two of them sat quietly together, with Mei being afraid to ask questions and Zhang too embarrassed to reach out.

I moved Mei next to Julissa, a sweet, outgoing Puerto Rican young woman, who had also moved to the United States just a few years before. Julissa brought light to Mei, and Mei opened up so much by the end of that year. I would see them chatting in the hallways or sometimes eating lunch together outside. This revised pairing was critical in helping Mei feel more comfortable in our space. Further, having cross-race/ethnic friends during adolescence is associated with more positive attitudes about peers of other races and ethnicities (Knifsend & Juvonen, 2013).

When it came time to facilitate book clubs, I kept this same level of intention when thinking about our groupings. I thought about my students' reading and English levels—and the levels of support and connection youth could provide each other.

This work is especially critical for emergent bi- and multilingual learners, as we want to honor our students' linguistic assets while also building their speaking and listening literacies. Saddleback Educational Publishing and Lee & Low Books have been instrumental in this work. Writing for students who are new to English and are reading at lower Lexile levels, these publishers provide texts that portray multilingual and multicultural adolescent characters. They offer fiction and nonfiction that focus on a variety of topics, from STEM to SEL, for tweens to teens. Other supports include texts with visuals and accompanying audio, and books written in languages from Korean to Tagalog.

For students such as Mei, we can offer book clubs in and out of class that focus on topics like being the new student or on topics about relationship-building. Further, we can provide texts that are written closer to their reading level so that they can experience success, while also thinking about ways they can develop connections within their new communities. At the same time, we can encourage students to read texts in their first language or offer them audio supports to listen and follow along as they read. On the website is a list of middle and high school texts that center issues of relationships.

As a specific example, *New Kid* (Craft, 2019) focuses on the challenges of creating and maintaining friendships in middle school. In this graphic novel, 7th-grader Jordan is an artist, but instead of going to an art school, his parents send him to private school, where he is one of the few young people of color. For the book group who is reading this text, after reading about Jordan's first day at his new school, we could offer the following questions to encourage conversations around relationship-building while also centering social awareness:

- How would you describe Jordan's relationship with his family? In what ways do his parents advocate for him? What kinds of advice do they offer? Do you agree or disagree with that advice? *(relationship-building)*
- How do you think Jordan's parents make him feel? *(perspective-taking)* How would you feel if you were Jordan? *(empathy)*
- What do you do if you disagree with members of your family? *(relationship-building)*
- What are some of the cultural differences that Jordan experiences at his new school? In what ways does he experience stereotyping and bullying from his peers and teachers? What kinds of labels are placed on Jordan and the other students of color at his school? *(critical consciousness)*
- Why does Jordan feel lost and alone? *(perspective-taking)* How might you feel if you were in Jordan's shoes? Have you experienced this feeling while in school? *(empathy)*
- How can we make friends if we are in a new space? How can we help others to feel safe and included in our school? *(relationship-building)*. What can we do to help advocate for others in our school? *(critical consciousness)*

These kinds of questions help students think critically about the text and help them to consider ways that their lives intersect with the characters. Students can grapple with the textual events and character emotions while also thinking about how they can inspire change within their own communities. In responding to these questions, students are also asked to be vulnerable, talk about their relationships, and discuss how they can connect with others, especially when in new spaces.

We must remember, however, that if we want these conversations to help students build relationships with each other, we need to support them. This means continuing with those opening rituals where we ask students about themselves before beginning our book clubs; it means providing mini-lessons to help students engage with one another; it means, as facilitators, modeling our own vulnerabilities by telling our stories as well; and it means asking students to reflect on their performance in the group.

When dealing with sensitive issues like relationship-building, we might ask students, either in writing or in speaking, to reflect on their participation in book club:

- Describe a time where you took a risk or when you were vulnerable in today's book club. How did that make you feel?
- Describe a time when you supported another student in book club. How did that make you feel?
- Describe a time when you connected with another student during your conversations. How did that make you feel?
- Did you experience any conflict today? How did you handle that?
- Part of being in book club is building relationships with each other. For your next session, what can you do to improve your connections to others?

Book clubs help students develop critical skills such as social awareness and relationship building. Next we consider our last piece of social development: enhancing students' sense of agency. Before we turn in this direction, however, let's pause and reflect on our template.

Centering Students' Social Development in Book Clubs	
What are your students' strengths and assets when thinking about their social development (i.e., social awareness and developing relationships)? What support do they need?	
What strategies, tools, and questions can you use to support students' social awareness?	What strategies, tools, and questions can you use to support students' development of relationships?

HOW CAN WE USE BOOK CLUBS TO
IMPACT STUDENTS' SENSE
OF AGENCY?

Today's world is fraught with inequities, controversies, and divisions, which young people witness and experience daily in their lives and through social media and the news. Youth are impacted by various injustices, from climate change to discrimination based on their gender, race, ability, language, sexuality, and other identity markers that have been marginalized and oppressed for centuries. As facilitators, we are naive to think we can bury our heads in the sand and avoid tough conversations. Worse, we are negligent if we do not provide young people with spaces to develop strategies to confront injustices and inequities. By developing skills such as social awareness and relationship building, we can engage in these discussions through more healing-centered and courageous approaches, where students begin to appreciate diversities and multiple perspectives, empathize with others, and most importantly, see themselves as agents for change (Simmons, 2019).

Ginwright and James (2002) describe this pedagogical approach as social justice youth development—a critical part of social-emotional learning that is often overlooked—where we create spaces for youth to analyze, challenge, and respond to imbalances of power in their lives and communities. In this way, we still consider our students' assets, but we take the work a step further in helping them to become agents of change. In embracing this approach, Ginwright and James (2002) suggest that we incorporate the following when developing youth agency:

- ensure that students' identities and communities are central to the work;
- center youth culture, focusing on current issues that impact and interest our students;
- analyze imbalances of power within various social relationships;
- focus on systemic change that critiques policies and institutions within our schools and local, national, and global contexts; and
- encourage collective action.

Before delving into what social justice youth development looks like in book clubs, I want us to pause and think about *why* we are doing this work, work that is embedded in emancipatory, justice, and equity-based practices (Love, 2019; Simmons, 2019). Why is this approach important for our students? I'd like us to reflect on who we are, what brings us here, and what we hope for; we must also consider what we are scared of, what we believe will get in the way, and what will be our challenges.

Establishing and Developing Our Own and Our Students' Sense of Agency	
Why is it important to integrate texts and conversations around social justice? Why is it important for your students to grapple with these topics?	What has been your own history with integrating social justice work into your personal and professional lives?
What do you hope this work will accomplish for you and your students?	What scares you about this work? What will be the challenges? What will get in the way?

I've talked a lot about what brings me to this work and my own educational practices and histories with justice and equity-based approaches to education. I've also talked about what I hope this work will do—and what I've *seen* this work do for young people. But it hasn't been easy. I've had white students push back and their parents complain. I've had white students change their ELA class to another teacher because of my orientations. I've had teachers leave my professional development sessions. During the pandemic, for example, I provided an online training on culturally sustaining literacy practices for emergent bi- and multilingual learners, using *All American Boys* (Reynolds & Kiely, 2015) as a model text for teaching students literacy skills while also considering their sense of agency. A woman wrote in the chat, "Is this a social justice lesson or a literacy lesson? This is the kind of indoctrination ruining our schools."

Despite my best zoom filter, my cheeks on that screen flushed red. I felt the familiar rattled butterflies of anxiety in my stomach. But I took a deep breath and explained that my students wanted to read about racism in their country and learn more about the #Blacklivesmatter movement. They also wanted to see themselves in the text, and they wanted to learn about youth who were advocating for racial justice.

My students at the time—all attending school in an alternative education district, all older adolescents who had not experienced academic "success" in their traditional schools—also had finished an entire book—for many, for the first time. They wrote two- to three-page narratives, using the book as a model for writing about their own acts of agency—again, for many, for the first time.

We cannot deny racism, sexism, and ableism; we cannot deny homo-, trans-, xeno-, and Islamophobias. Ignoring these inequities does not serve our students—our students of color and our white students.

I tell you about my failures and successes, my challenges and fears to be vulnerable. To share that I know the path is not easy. But we must remember that our students matter most. And we must listen to what matters to them. In keeping their well-being in our hearts and minds—as our first priorities—our path to justice becomes less difficult to climb.

So let's now talk about what this work can look like, specifically in book clubs, particularly as we take on and center issues of power, privilege, and various inequities and injustices. One scaffolded way to begin the conversations is through reading shorter texts that exemplify what it looks like to become involved as youth in social movements and what it looks like to advocate for ourselves and others. On the website are suggestions for informational texts that describe the incredibly important work of youth activists who fight gun violence, who bring awareness to climate change, and who organize for Black and Indigenous lives. Utilizing shorter readings in small groups provides models of young people who work to bring change into the world. To guide students' thinking, we might ask our reading groups to consider the following questions, which continue to help build students' perspective-taking and empathy skills—while also encouraging them to think about their own sense of agency:

- What are these youth advocating for? Why is this topic so important to them and their communities? *(perspective-taking)*
- What strategies do they use to bring about change? *(agency)*
- What kinds of relationships and collaborations do they need to be successful? *(relationship-building)*
- How do you think this kind of activism makes youth feel? *(empathy)*
- In what ways have you organized for change or advocated for others? What strategies did you use? *(agency)*

To supplement these article reading groups, I'd recommend watching videos of youth activists, several of which are posted on the website, and bringing in guest speakers who are local youth organizers.

Young adult literature is another effective method for developing students' sense of agency. To explore this genre, we might weave in critical literacy, a tool that helps youth analyze imbalances of power and inequities within texts. Critical literacy asks students to think about ways in which texts are culturally, historically, and politically situated (Luke, 2012; Morrell, 2008). In using critical literacy, we foster students' abilities to critique and transform "dominant ideologies, cultures, economies, institutions, and political systems" (Luke, 2012, p. 5). Further, critical literacy pushes young readers beyond the text, asking them to both read the word and their world, as it connects to the events and characters (Freire & Macedo, 1987).

An important part of critical literacy is also asking students to consider who they are as readers—how their identities, languages, literacies, abilities, and lived experiences impact how they make meaning of the text. Some of my most exciting book clubs have been heterogeneous in terms of students' gender, racial and ethnic identities, sexualities, and abilities. Once safety has been established, I encourage students to discuss how their interpretations differ based on who they are and what they bring to the text. These conversations provide students with multiple ideas for how texts can be interpreted and experienced, making the reading process much more fluid by encouraging students to consider their positionalities.

This approach is especially important for white students, as they can use texts to think about the characters' experiences and how their own positions of power and privilege play out in their communities. In doing this work, we can ask students to lean into that discomfort, acknowledging their own complicity and benefits from living within oppressive systems that privilege whiteness and other aspects of our identities, such as being middle class, cisgender, and able-bodied (Staley & Leonardi, 2016). When we ask students to dig into that discomfort and acknowledge their complicity within oppressive systems, they often become stronger agents within social justice efforts (Staley & Leonardi, 2016). On the website is a list of resources, from picture books to adolescent literature, to help white students think about their privilege and ways they can leverage their position to advocate for and with marginalized communities.

For white teachers who are doing work around white privilege, we must remember that we too have to continue to not only reflect on our positionality but also to model that reflection and action for our students so that they know we are committed to justice and equity, and for our white students, so that they have models of what this work can look like.

Critical literacy can also come into play for facilitators who feel the constraints of curriculum mandates and pressures to teach more canonical texts. We can ask students to participate in different kinds of reading (Borsheim-Black, Macaluso, & Petrone, 2014; Janks, 2010), such as analyzing the author's intentions, especially in context of the time period; connecting the text to their own current lived experiences; and analyzing *against* the text by interrogating the assumptions, values, and positions presented by the author.

Regardless of the texts we use, we can create questions grounded in critical literacy by keeping the following tenets in mind (Luke & Woods, 2009; Riley, 2015):

- Ask students to analyze the ideologies in the text, specifically power imbalances and the marginalization of communities.
- Leverage empathy-building and integration of multiple perspectives.
- Center the voices and lived experiences of marginalized communities.

- Connect analysis to current events and the lived experiences of youth.
- Emphasize that literacies are sociopolitical actions that can be used to inspire change.
- Emphasize that literacies are humanizing processes that encourage aesthetic and emotional responses and interactions.
- Emphasize that literacy engagements are collective and democratic.

These tenets are suggestions we can use to plan our book club intentions and ones that can be explicitly shared with students. They are not meant to be a formula (Luke, 2000), as the work of critical literacy should be organic and grounded in students' needs and interests.

Let's now look at a model for what this can look like in our book clubs. Oftentimes, I teach critical literacy through the use of lenses. If I want to center issues around race and racism with my middle school students, for example, I would first be sure to provide choices on what they want to read, including texts that are written by authors of color and that focus on racial justice. Let's return to *New Kid* (Craft, 2019) as an example.

To scaffold the work of critical lenses, I would first talk to my students about their understanding of race and racism and how that has impacted their lives and communities. We might look at multiple definitions of race and racism and come to shared understandings about what these words mean. We might read excerpts from *A Kid's Book About Systemic Racism* (Thierry, 2020) or *This Book Is Anti-Racist* (Jewell, 2020) to build on students' background knowledge and to enhance their discourse for talking about these issues.

It's also important to discuss how difficult the conversations might be. As a white woman, I speak directly to my own discomfort, talking about my whiteness and the privilege that brings. This vulnerability helps students not feel alone—and it models the importance of risk-taking and that we are all continually growing. Kay (2018) suggests that we use the following agreements with our students to help make them feel safer when coming to these discussions:

- "We agree that nobody deserves to be hurt by their peers" in our community.
- "We agree . . . that each other's hopes, anxieties, and vulnerabilities are worth both our attention and our empathy" (p. 259).

Once agreements are established, I talk to students about reading critically, specifically about reading texts with a lens. I use the metaphor of putting on a pair of glasses. When we put those on, we begin to see the word *and* the world in different ways. Applying critical theories allows students to focus on a text with a new perspective. Further, applying critical theories puts the power of meaning-making into our students' hands, with the lenses offering them opportunities for agency as readers.

To introduce reading critically with a lens toward race and racism, I might start with picture books as a way to scaffold the process before moving on to more complex texts. On the first reading, I want students to just read for story, character, questions, and connections they have. I want them to experience the text organically and share those initial reactions within their book club. On the second read, I would ask them to think about what we know about race and racism and then put that lens on as we read the text again. We then share our interpretations with this new eye toward racial justice. If needed, I keep guiding questions ready:

- What is my own identity and does it intersect with the text? How does my racialized identity impact my reading?
- What message is the author offering to us about race and racism?
- What kinds of injustices is the character experiencing?
- In what ways does our main character resist and confront racism? How do the characters work collectively with others to resist and confront racism?
- What joy does the author bring us through these narratives? Where do we see hope?
- In what ways can we emulate resistance, agency, and advocacy within our own lives? How can we collectively do this work?

Once we've practiced this lens with picture books, we can then move on to more challenging young adult literature, with me continuing to keep these guiding questions in my pocket to help students apply a critical race lens to their textual interpretations.

On the website are other critical lenses that we can apply in our book clubs, including feminism, LatCrit (Latinx Critical Race Theory, CRT), Asian American CRT, Tribal CRT, DisCrit and ableism, intersectionality, Marxism, and queer theories. I have offered student-friendly definitions and tenets for each theory and instructional articles to help guide you in the process and see models. In addition, I provide young adult literature (YAL) that pairs well with these theories along with supplemental texts.

Based on your students and your school, you will introduce these theories in different ways. For example, a teacher friend of mine feared teaching the concept of "feminism" with her students because of the climate in her school district. Yet, she taught *Speak* (Anderson, 1999) in an 8th-grade classroom through a feminist lens, asking students to explore the gender inequities in the text but never using the word "feminism" in her class. I have another educator friend who taught *George* (Gino, 2017), a narrative of a tween transgender student, to her 6th-grade classroom, where she talked about terms such as "gender norms" and "transphobia"—and yet she never explicitly used the term "queer theory." With my high school students just this year, I explicitly taught queer theory and critical race theory, as my school climate allowed for such conversations and students were interested in the topics. There is no prescription for how to teach critical theories, and your approaches will vary based on getting to know your students and attending to your school context.

Just note that critical theories can be taught and used across all grade levels, and we can do that work based on meeting students where they are. In using these lenses, ultimately we want to empower students to view texts from different perspectives. How we talk about these lenses and what books we use may change, based on our context. If we are teaching in more conservative districts, the work may look very different, but that doesn't mean it cannot be done.

So what do critical lenses have to do with developing students' sense of agency? Applying theories to texts can be a place of liberation in that we offer students languages and opportunities for critique (hooks, 1991; Leonardo, 2004). Further, when we validate and listen to students who have experienced discrimination and oppression, when we offer them texts that mirror these experiences, and when we provide them with lenses to help them understand these experiences from a systemic perspective, we can use these instructional moments to help them develop their identities as empowered readers and change agents (if they aren't already both).

When we finish our books, we can then use assessments that connect to social justice. Perhaps you are a science teacher and you are doing book clubs on climate change. Once students are done reading those texts, they can create public service announcements about ways to engage in environmental justice. Terrific work has also been done in youth participatory action research (i.e., Caraballo & Lyiscott, 2020; Morrell, 2008), where students conduct research grounded in their inquiries. We can also integrate justice-based community projects. After reading *Seedfolks* (Fleischman, 2004), my students and I collaborated with our science teacher and our school neighbors to cultivate a garden. After reading *Slake's Limbo* (Holman, 1986), my students and I volunteered at our local shelter for people who are unhoused. And after participating in a series of book clubs about abuse, my students and I collaborated with our art teacher to create brochures for young people about how they can get help if they feel in harm's way. Those were all donated to a local youth counseling center.

The impact of book clubs on students' literacies and social-emotional learning is evident. If we do the work in mindful ways, attuning to the sociopolitical contexts of our students and their youth cultures, we can engage students not only in reading a variety of texts that they *actually* enjoy, but we can use these spaces to demonstrate that we value all the diversities they bring. We can also use these spaces to help them develop relationships with each other—and those outside of our space—all while channeling their energies to be agents of change.

Enacting critical literacy and discussing agency and advocacy with our students will be a struggle—and we will need to take risks. In doing so, we will most certainly trip up and falter. But the work is important to our students and for our communities if we want to see a more inclusive and humanizing world. I ask that, despite the challenges, you not give up—that you continue to educate yourself and get feedback from your students, reaching out to others who can help you in collective transformation. For now, using our template, let's pause and think about what this work might look like in your future book clubs.

What are your students' strengths and assets when thinking about their sense of agency?	
What are areas where students can use support when developing their sense of agency?	What strategies, tools, and questions can you use to support your students' sense of agency?

CHAPTER 7

Engaging With Youth Families and in Digital Spaces

It's the end of the school year, and I'm doing my best to collect all the books that students have borrowed throughout the semester. Students are writing their final reflections on their literacy growth while I check to see which books still need to be returned. Students reach into their book bags, pulling out texts and returning them to my desk. I notice that Asia has quite a few books that she has not brought back to our class library. I call her over.

"Asia," I whisper. "What happened to all those books you read this year?"

"Miss, I'm sorry," she says with a grin. "But they look really good in our house. My mom got us a bookshelf and everything. And they're all there—and she reads them and my cousins read them and my friends. We've even been getting more from Barnes and Noble and now when everybody comes over, we share the books and talk about 'em. It's like book club in my house!"

I can't help but laugh and shake my head, immediately thinking how my principal is going to reprimand me again for all the books that need to be replaced. But I don't care. Asia and her family are connecting through literature and conversation, and there is no way I am going to remove those resources from her home. This last chapter will focus on how we can expand the sphere of book clubs from beyond the brick and mortar of schools and into students' homes, both through networking with their families and by engaging in innovative digital spaces so that we can enhance our reach into the possibilities of youth-centered book clubs.

HOW CAN BOOK CLUBS BE INCLUSIVE OF OUR STUDENTS' FAMILIES?

Research tells us time and again that adolescents benefit when we collaborate with their families—when we make connections from home to school. When families are involved, we see an increase in student achievement, motivation, self-esteem, and attendance (Wiseman, 2011). Studying the families and experiences of African American youth, Hucks (2014) calls for the need to create educational models of *collective achievement*, where we envision and enact ways to work together with families to support students. As facilitators of book clubs, this means valuing our students' families as intellectual and cultural assets with the goal of meeting our students' needs and providing valuable information for our own instruction and support systems (Rodriguez, 2013).

Auerbach (2012) asks us to consider this collective path by building authentic partnerships with families, where we cultivate relationship-building, prioritize dialogue, and share the power in creating school spaces that are socially just, inclusive, and democratic. To this end, when planning for book clubs, we must incorporate the goals of our students' families and build systems that are equitable and that reach beyond academics to students' social and emotional growth as well. When we interact with families in mutually engaging ways, we can create communities that are responsive to and sustaining of our students' cultures, languages, communities, and literacies, ultimately working toward achievement that points to both academic and social-emotional development.

Thus, regardless of our role in schools, one of our goals should be to provide spaces where families feel welcomed, valued, and integrated in our larger school communities and within our smaller book club processes. Unfortunately, studies have demonstrated that multilingual families, families from low socioeconomic areas, and families of color often do not feel included in schools, due to cultural and racial issues and feelings of mistrust of educational institutions that have not served them in the past (Kuperminc, Darnell, & Alvarez-Jimenez, 2008). As book club facilitators, we must reach out to our students' families, informing them of our work and listening to their hopes and concerns. We also must strive to differentiate how we engage with families. Like our students, families are different, with various obligations, languages, work schedules, and historical experiences with schooling. Asking families *how* they want to be involved in our school communities allows us to create experiences that meet their needs. Like our work with students, our efforts in family engagement must also be humanizing and culturally affirming, where we value and include our families' cultures and languages. As such, we must unpack traditional methods for participation and think more inclusively and broadly of diverse communicative and connective practices. When we are intentional about including families' cultural funds of knowledge and assets (Moll, 1992), then we begin to truly utilize the robust resources *all* of our families bring.

A large part of this work is avoiding deficit language to describe students' families (Gabriel, Roxas, & Becker, 2017; Gorski, 2013; Valencia, 2010). Guerra and Nelson (2013) found that deficit thinking and language lead culturally, linguistically, and economically diverse families to feel as if they are problems in schools. Peralta (2019) found that schools overall tend to underestimate the commitments and abilities of families to contribute to students' academic development, particularly in literacies. If we are more informed about our families' circumstances and build authentic relationships, then we can better serve both our families and our students.

What can this look like in our book club spaces? First, research tells us that when youth share the books they are reading with their families, they are given increased opportunities to talk about texts, enhancing new connections with their loved ones (Ivey & Johnston, 2018). For one of my informal book club assignments, I ask students to share their text with one family member or person in their community. They then write a short piece of their choice about the discussions they had, describing what it felt like to talk about books with others outside of school. In many cases, students have come back to school asking if they can borrow their book club text a little longer so that their family member can have an opportunity to read it as well.

I also send home letters to families about what book clubs are and the purpose of doing such work. I share a brief overview of the evidence-based research for book clubs, a calendar of our meetings, and descriptions of the text options. Being transparent about our approaches is critical in keeping families informed about what we are doing and why. I also use this opportunity to ask families how they would like to be involved, from donating texts to attending our book club celebrations.

In terms of larger school activities, you might consider collaborating with others at your school to hold a literacy night or weekend event, which can help cultivate relationships with families while offering opportunities for literacy celebrations. Librarians, for example, can provide library tours and recommend various multilingual texts that range from fiction to nonfiction for adolescent and adult audiences alike. Families can also engage in "mini-book clubs," where they read a short story or poem together and engage in the book club process to get a sense of what these activities feel like. Family literacy events also provide wonderful opportunities for students to share the books they are reading in book clubs. During these events to accommodate family needs, I recommend offering food and prizes along with childcare for those students with younger siblings.

We also want to be vigilant about reaching out to families right at the beginning of the year to learn about our students' literacy practices at home, while also discovering what our families' goals are for their children. On the website is a sample letter I send to families along with a brief survey that gathers information I need to understand my students better, while also ascertaining how I can improve my instruction to meet their needs. All of these modes of communication are always translated by support staff so that the materials are accessible to our multilingual families.

I also get input from students themselves. Thus, also at the beginning of the year, I give students an inventory to get a sense of who they are. Here, I ask them to provide me with information they feel comfortable sharing about their families: Who lives at home with you? Who should I call if I want to share a celebration or concern? Any advice for how to best communicate with your family? This information is critical, especially when I want to celebrate students' involvement in book club or when I might need support from home if a student is struggling in these spaces.

Our work does not stop at the start of the semester, however, because we want to ensure that, as with our students, we create relationships with families throughout the year by building what Llopart and Esteban-Guitart (2018) call *confianza,* or mutual trust. One way to build that trust is by being transparent about what we do in our classrooms, as is evidenced with the book club informational letter described previously. In addition, when I was a full-time classroom teacher, my students and I collaboratively created a class newsletter once a quarter for their families to celebrate our work. This was a great way in which to highlight the texts that students read in book clubs. You might also opt for a class website that families can access that includes videos of student presentations or clips from students participating in book clubs. Another alternative is to send out book recommendations from your school or classroom libraries so that families can see what is available. This transfer of resources is not unilateral, however. Several of my students have brought in books from their homes to share, and many of those have become text options for our book clubs.

I also ask my students to fill in their address on four "praise postcards." Every quarter, I send home one postcard to each student's family, praising something they did in class or in book club that was cause for celebration. Students love receiving these in the mail, as do their families. Sometimes, students will even "request" when I should send these home: "Jody, I have a basketball game I want to go to next Friday with friends. Any chance my praise postcard could go out this week? Did you see how great I was in book club yesterday?"

One year that I did this, a student asked me to call his mother about his postcard. I asked him why, and he responded, "She only gets bad phone calls about me. She doesn't believe you really sent it."

This comment made me sad for my students' families in that we often only communicate when something is wrong, and this is not the kind of one-sided, deficit mode of communication we want to use with families. Praise postcards are just one way to do this, and a simple email to families will work too.

In my previous high school, we also shifted to student-led family conferences once per semester, which resulted in engaging students much more in the process, giving them opportunities to articulate and advocate for their learning (Cronin, 2016). These conferring approaches differ from family-teacher discussions by placing students at the center, where they come prepared with materials and are offered opportunities to reflect on their learning. In doing so, students take responsibility and ownership for their literacies, engaging in goal-setting and assessment review in a more transparent process. These experiences are also beneficial for our multilingual families, allowing students to lead conferences in their home language.

You might also consider having family book clubs, where families are invited to participate in their own reading groups with faculty, staff, and other families. Texts can range from young adult literature to books that center issues important to students' families. These forums can be done in the schools themselves, in local community centers, or remotely. Van Duinen, Hamilton, and Rumohr-Voskuil (2017), for example, created book clubs for mothers and daughters, where once a month participants gathered together to discuss and disrupt dominant discourse around adolescence.

Similarly, in Philadelphia, the Caucus of Working Educators and the Teacher Action Group developed an ongoing summer reading series that involves families, teachers, community members, librarians, and other youth development professionals. Participants read different texts to raise political consciousness and then collectively use knowledge from the books to enact change within their communities (Riley & Cohen, 2018). The book clubs meet in various community spaces and independent bookstores, speaking to issues related to educational justice. For those participants who cannot attend the sessions, running blogs are kept so that they can still engage in the work. The most powerful outcome of these book clubs is that they have led to leadership-building and many of the groups continue to meet throughout the year. Inspired by the texts, these organizing committees engage in activism around such issues as housing justice, restorative practices, combating white supremacy, supporting LGBTQ communities, and immigration.

Families are incredible resources, and through our differentiated, humanizing, and culturally sustaining approaches, we can collaborate with them to meet the needs of our students in much more intentional and holistic ways. Pause for a moment and strategize ways you might engage families in your own future book clubs.

What strategies might you use to engage families in your book club/s?

WHAT DO BOOK CLUBS LOOK LIKE IN DIGITAL SPACES?

In March 2020, due to the COVID-19 pandemic, all schools in New York City—and across the nation—closed their doors, and classes were moved to online spaces. Frightened by the virus and unprepared to teach or learn remotely, both teachers and students found the transition challenging. At the time, I worked in an alternative school district with older adolescents, many of whom did not have access to technology and were recent immigrants and refugees separated from their families. Concerned about their well-being, our resourceful counselors did their best to find these young people and ensure that they were emotionally and physically safe in a city that was brutalized by the virus.

In the beginning, we struggled, as most schools did. Many of our students did not have Internet access or computers. Teachers did not know how to use Google Classroom or Zoom. And for several weeks, education and connection just stopped.

It was a traumatic time for us all, but especially for those students who were struggling economically. Most of our students had full-time jobs, many of which they relied on to pay their rent. Many lost those jobs as restaurants and stores shut their doors indefinitely. Socially, students were now isolated from each other, fearful to leave their homes, as they heard sirens raging from early morning to late at night. Emotionally, they were alone, afraid, and uncertain about their future.

We knew we had to reach our students in innovative ways, and now more than ever, use our instruction to not only bolster their literacies but to help them cope in a world that seemed to be at its end. As a school community, we had to collectively find ways to bring joy to their homes—and we did so through book clubs.

You've read about some of these reading groups in Chapter 5; the young women who read *With the Fire on High* (Acevedo, 2019) and the young men who read *Written in the Stars* (Saeed, 2016) are just two examples. During this time, I even reached out to students I taught in Amsterdam the previous year and connected them with my U.S. students. We had international conversations about their shared love of science fiction and activism, starting with our first book, *Scythe* (Shusterman, 2017).

While the pandemic changed all of our lives significantly, this time offered us unique opportunities to learn how to reach students through digital spaces. According to the Bureau of Labor Statistics (2019), adolescents ages 15–24 spend on average 7 minutes per day reading for enjoyment, yet they engage with media and digital literacies for over 3 hours of leisure per day. Further, a Pew study found that 85% of teens use YouTube, 72% Instagram, 69% Snapchat, and 51% Facebook (Anderson & Jiang, 2018). Pew's research also discovered that 95% have access to smartphones and 88% have access to a desktop or laptop, with 45% saying they were online "almost constantly."

Our students come to us with such rich background knowledge and experience with technology. To ignore those assets is to miss out on vital home-school connections. Students are engaged with technologies and literacies, and we can use those gifts to bridge the divides between home and school.

Let's first discuss technology as it connects to expanding students' literacies. For one, we can provide books through digital methods on a variety of devices. I have several students who read books on their phones, especially as they commute on the subway. One male student explained, "Miss, I can't be caught reading a book on the train! But I can hide it by reading on my phone."

By reading texts digitally—whether on phones or tablets—students can acquire definitions to words they don't know and access audio versions to help build their fluency and comprehension. Digital devices also allow students to annotate texts, for example, using the notes feature to keep track of personal connections and questions. They can then easily access their notes when they come to book club.

We can also use digital tools for our literacy assessments. Instead of those traditional book talks, why not have students create book trailers and place them on YouTube? Students can also use software such as iMovie to create digital stories and poetry inspired by the texts they read (Greene, 2016). To engage in their critical consciousness, students can create public service announcements (PSAs) that address particular issues raised in their texts. For example, if a book club read *El Deafo* (Bell, 2014), where the main character is deaf and feels isolated in her school, students could research how to support youth with hearing challenges and then use that knowledge to create a PSA to bring awareness while developing strategies for supporting deaf communities. Students could also create storyboards or collaborate on collective zines to teach others about the critical concerns raised in their texts. The opportunities and options are limitless!

As for digital book clubs, research has demonstrated the power of these spaces, particularly as these forums provide innovation and engaging contexts for rich discussions (Bowers-Campbell, 2011; Schreuder & Savitz, 2020). Greene (2016), for example, used online book clubs to read *Push* (Sapphire, 1997); in these sessions, young people engaged in critical literacies around issues of identity construction and social justice. Similarly, Colwell, Woodward, and Hutchison (2018) found online book clubs not only promoted shared learning but allowed students to make personal connections and to understand diverse perspectives.

Some school districts use digital book clubs as an opportunity to increase summer reading. During the summer, students often experience a learning loss. On average, student achievement can decline over the summer by one month to one year of a school-year learnings; the extent of this loss is greater as students get older (Quinn & Polikoff, 2017). These losses are even more pronounced for students from low-income households and students of color. One innovative practice then is to offer summer online digital book clubs.

So what do these spaces look like in practice? First, digital book clubs can be offered through synchronous or asynchronous forums (Polleck & Smith, 2021). Regardless of the option you choose, survey students first to learn about their interests and needs. In the past, I have used Google Forms to find out critical information—from students' demographics to their reading preferences. This survey should also ask students about their needs, including how they prefer to read (i.e., tablet, phone, or computer) and necessary supports (i.e., books, technology, audiobooks, books in students' first languages). I can also use this tool to assess students' background knowledge on technology and digital platforms. Most importantly, digital surveys help me group students based on their shared interests. As an example, one group of students wanted to read science fiction, so I provided them with book options that centered social justice and reflected their neurodiversities and sexual, gender, racial, and ethnic diversities. Book choices included *On the Edge of Gone* (Duyvis, 2016), *Dread Nation* (Ireland, 2018), *Scythe* (Shusterman, 2017), *Shadowshaper* (Older, 2016), and *Huntress* (Lo, 2012). Students then voted on what they wanted to read and created a schedule for their reading and meetings.

If conducting synchronous book clubs, once groups are formed, as the facilitator you can determine with your students what that schedule will be. If these are out-of-classroom experiences, perhaps students can meet online after school or during the day for summer book clubs. Digital platforms such as Zoom or Kumospace are terrific tools to group young people so that you can float in and out of the breakout rooms to see how they are doing. With digital tools such as these, we can even connect students from all over the world, as I did with the *Scythe* reading group, where students from Amsterdam and New York connected once a week to talk about their international perspectives on the text and life during the pandemic (Polleck & Smith, 2021).

Digital book clubs can be facilitated asynchronously as well. In this case, youth read books on their own but connect to each other at different times. Stewart-Mitchell (2020) connected students in Grades 4 through 12 across her district of 32 schools. Students were able to chat about their books through blogging, and, in doing so, Stewart-Mitchell found that youth were more engaged in the work and felt more accountable about what they wrote because of the authentic audience. Similarly, Smith (2020) used Flipgrid for his digital book clubs. In this case, Smith videoed himself using the platform, offering questions for readers to respond to. Then once per week, at a time of their convenience, readers would video record their textual responses. Other members of the book club could then leave either written comments or videos responding to those initial reactions. Practitioners and researchers of asynchronous book clubs find that these forums allow readers time to think about their responses before sharing and provide time for them to take special care in their textual analysis and their responses to others (Bowers-Campbell, 2011; Smith, 2020).

Stewart-Mitchell (2020) also recommends teacher modeling for asynchronous spaces to help students communicate with one another in humanizing ways. Her guidance includes asking youth to write 3 Cs and a Q when responding on their blogs: a compliment about the post; a comment that is relevant to the post; a connection to either the text, self, or world; and a question to keep the conversations going. Students also should have options to respond with GIFs, images, and links to Twitter, YouTube, and Instagram to demonstrate in various ways how they connect with the texts and each other.

Students can also use other digital tools, besides Flipgrid and blogging, to respond to each other. I've used such platforms as Padlet and Google Jamboard. You can even use Google Slides, asking each book group to create a different slide collaboratively representing the major themes of their texts. Then the book clubs can share their slides and offer comments to each other, making connections among the different texts.

Regardless of how you decide to utilize digital tools and spaces, they can offer incredibly powerful bridges for youth readers: from home to school, from student to student, across distance and difference. Take some time to strategize ways you might include digital tools and spaces in your own book clubs.

How might you infuse digital tools and spaces into your book club(s)?

QR Code for Chapter 7 Resources

Epilogue
Centering Joy in Book Club Spaces

We have just finished reading *Jason and Kyra* (Davidson, 2005), and the young women in our book club are discussing how Kyra makes a decision not to have sex with her boyfriend, Jason. Tia praises her choice, sharing, "I'm the kind of person where even if you were sexually active before, you have to give up sex to be with me."

"Same!" Betsy, Sofia, and Fay agree simultaneously.

Sofia clarifies, "If they love you, they should wait until you're ready."

"If you are pressuring me about sex, then you don't respect me," shares Tia. "You know, I have a friend who is sexually active, and she's not just sexually active with one person. I don't think that's a problem. I'm not going to be sexually active but if you want to do it, that's your business. It's not mine."

"Yeah," Fay agrees. "Just be sure to use the right stuff. That's why they made those protections."

"Exactly!" Tia confirms. "No judgments and no slut-shaming here, but she told me that she did it without a condom, and she keeps doing it without a condom and I'm like that's stupid. She did it three times!"

"Three?" shouts Joy. "Oh yeah, she's pregnant."

Worried the group may spiral into judging this young woman's choices, I interject, "I want to commend Tia's awareness of judgments and slut-shaming. It's important we lift each other up as opposed to bringing each other down. Since the person we're discussing is not here, how about we talk about what we learn from Kyra in the book—and what can we learn from each other—in terms of making decisions about our partners to ensure we are emotionally and physically safe?"

The young women nod in understanding, with Tia switching the focus from her friend to a character: "I remember when we read *Forever*. She wasn't using condoms."

"*And* he had a VD," adds Sofia. "Like the clap or something? What's that?"

"It's slang for gonorrhea," I explain.

"Man! There are a whole bunch of different ones," Fay exclaims. "How can you keep track?"

The young women start rattling off various sexually transmitted diseases, from chlamydia to herpes. Joy interrupts, pleading, "What do we do with all these diseases out there?"

"Use a condom!" Betsy insists.

"Not even," says Tia. "Isn't herpes skin-to-skin contact? The condom only goes so far."

"Aren't there pills that make them go away?" Sofia asks. "And what about warts? I've heard of them too. You get warts on your fingers sometimes but that's not the same. I used to have one, but now it's a callus."

The young women then begin to discuss various methods of contraception, from dental dams to diaphragms. Sophia exclaims, "Oh my god, so many methods! And guys only have condoms? They don't have anything else, and we have all these! Why do we have to suffer so much?"

"And we didn't even get into birth control pills or other things like Norplant," I say.

"Oh yeah, my sister had that," Joy comments.

"There's also Depo-Provera," I remind them. "Where you get a shot every three months."

"My friend is on that," Tia confirms.

Fay then braces her hands on the table, deep in thought, and hesitantly asks, "So what about—what is it? Lunesta?"

The girls all pause for a moment, considering her question until Tia shouts, "That's a sleeping pill! I mean the best contraception out there! Here baby, take your pill so you fall asleep, and we won't have to have sex!"

We all start laughing uncontrollably. Fay laughs so hard, she grips her stomach and falls out of her seat. Betsy reaches down to help her up, crying, "Girl, book club can*not* be beat."

Our book club eventually returns to the text. And afterward, I connect with my school social worker and read up on websites about how to best talk about sex with youth so that I am better prepared and informed about how to follow up with the young women.

In reflecting back now, I still chuckle thinking about this moment. I am also left with hope, seeing how book club inspired such critical inquiries around topics that mattered to young people, about how these spaces brought us together as readers and friends, and most importantly, how the books and conversations provided us with joy, laughter, and lightness that we so often overlook in our school communities.

While this is our final anecdote, as we approach the end of our literary and pedagogical journey, my hope is your travels with book clubs are just beginning. Beyond these book clubs, my hope is also that we can begin to see the possibilities for transformative experiences, from the small ripples of book clubs to the larger systemic waves that can be made to change school climate, ensuring that students are valued, included, and surrounded by humanizing pedagogies and support systems.

Book clubs can be viewed as a microcosm of what we ultimately want for our school communities. These kinds of spaces—that allow for hope, vulnerability, and connection—provide us forums for building community, tools for academic and social-emotional growth, and inspiration and strategies for social justice and critical consciousness building. The collective nature of book clubs, most importantly, gives us time to reflect and to act (Freire, 1993; hooks, 1994).

These spaces do not have to be limited to afterschool or ELA classrooms. Book clubs are forums that invite texts and discussions across all content boundaries. Our art teachers, for example, can read graphic novels to study the design and structure of the genre while also providing perspectives and strategies for social justice. Or perhaps our health and science teachers can read young adult novels that grapple with a variety of mental health issues as they intersect with the racialized and gendered identities of youth. In both of these examples, not only do students enrich their understanding of our discipline from art to health, but they also engage in conversations that allow for the inclusion of diverse perspectives and transformation of the ways we think about the world. In doing so, we can connect to meaningful projects linked to activism and social justice to engage students as agents of change.

As facilitators, we must continually support students in this work, remembering to mentor, teach, and collaborate in flexible, honest, vulnerable, and transparent ways. Further, we must facilitate with humility and grace, with constant reflection and revision as we work to improve our processes and methods. Kay (2018) reminds us that "lasting improvement requires dedication to the humbling cycle of practice and reflection" (p. 269). In being practitioners who are committed to humility, we engage in social justice, a never-ending process of both learning and unlearning (Tervalon & Murray-Garcia, 1998).

We must also remember we are not alone; through collaborating with our colleagues, students, and families, we can engage in the transformative work that leads to sustainable impact and change. At the same time, we need to reach outside of our school communities and continually grow, leaning into local, national, and global professional organizations to guide our work and diving into texts that offer us guidance and direction as we continue working in a variety of settings, from book clubs to larger local and national politics. When we are proactive about our professional learning, we can better serve our students, families, and communities (Ginwright, 2018).

So read a lot. Learn about your school communities through books and engage in texts about critical pedagogies. Talk about these issues with others. Also remember, we must be "scholars" of our students; we must get to know them and their families—and we must read texts that connect to those diverse languages, literacies, abilities, and cultures. Then, we need to take that learning and commit to our students, their families, and the larger context—disrupting inequitable systems and being an agent of change, alongside our students (Tanner, 2019). Love (2019) explains, "Pedagogy, regardless by name, is useless without teachers dedicated to challenging systemic oppression with intersectional social justice" (p. 19).

So what now? What can we do in the immediate future? Perhaps start your own book club with colleagues in your school and use that newly acquired knowledge—that discussion and collaboration—to enact changes within your communities. Or, start an afterschool or lunchtime student-led book club that centers their interests while providing them with time and space to engage in social justice work through collective action. And when you're ready, bring these book clubs to your classroom—saturating the community with literature that reflects students' identities, that engages youth in conversation, and that inspires them for agency.

Creating book clubs, small or large, for connection and advocacy will most certainly be arduous, but the risks are worth the benefits as we collectively work for equity within our school community and broader society. I've certainly made many mistakes along the way—and you will probably find many of them in this book—but after making these mistakes, we have to dust ourselves off and learn from them. Matias (2016) asks us to embrace this discomfort, especially as emotions are critical to "challenging dominant beliefs, social habits, and normative practices that sustain racism and social inequities, and in creating possibilities for individual and social transformation" (p. 40).

In 1857, abolitionist Frederick Douglass told us that "if there is no struggle, there is no progress," and 150 years later, our current abolitionist warrior Bettina Love (2019) tells us "to want freedom is to welcome struggle" (p. 9). Pedagogies and support systems grounded in equity are not easy, but they are a must.

Within this struggle, we must also remember to ground our work in love. Ginwright (2016) asks us to consider ourselves as "soul rebels," where we work on unraveling "conventional educational and political strategies" and embarking on journeys that allow us "to discover practices that heal and transform classrooms, organizations, and communities" (p. 5). Alternative approaches for student support, such as book clubs, cannot function or succeed without grounding in healing and in love. As facilitators we must come to groups with love, communicating that emotion, modeling what it looks like, so that these spaces become forums for collective healing and hope building.

Healing is entrenched in social justice. Through the texts and our conversations, we can radically imagine spaces for equity, collective hope, and critical action. Ginwright (2016) shares, "Social change begins in the heart, when teachers and activists declare an unapologetic and radical love for their communities and their young people" (p. 38).

Part of this process is also about loving and caring for ourselves. There may be moments of pain and frustration in facilitating book clubs, and there may be resistance to your vision of advocacy. It is in these moments that we must remember to love and take care of our own sense of well-being—for "if we are not whole for ourselves, we cannot be whole for our students" (Simmons, 2020a, p. 89).

Finally, intertwined with these last thoughts and closings, I will leave you with visions of joy. Joy for the texts and conversations; joy through the laughter and the friendships; joy in the imagining and creation of innovative, equitable spaces; and joy in the hope for our future. At just 14, Fay explained that book clubs—through the reading and conversations—can "give us visions for how we can see and be in the world." And though book clubs are small movements for inclusion and connection, ultimately I hope for you and your students that they will generate large leaps for transformation.

References

Abolitionist Teaching Network. (2020). *Guide for racial justice and abolitionist social and emotional learning.* Author.

Acevedo, E. (2019). *With the fire on high.* Quill Tree.

Ahmed, S. (2019). *Love, hate and other filters.* Soho Teen.

Ahmed, S. (2020). *Internment.* Little, Brown Books for Young Readers.

Alexie, S. (2009). *The absolutely true diary of a part-time Indian.* Little, Brown Books for Young Readers.

Alford, K. (2020). Explicitly teaching listening in the ELA curriculum: Why and how. *The English Journal, 109*(5), 22–29.

Ali, S. K. (2018). *Saints and misfits.* Simon & Schuster Books for Young Readers.

Alim, H. S. (2005). Critical language awareness in the United States: Revisiting issues and revising pedagogies in a resegregated society. *Educational Researcher, 34*(7), 24–31.

Alim, H. S., & Smitherman, G. (2012). *Articulate while Black: Barack Obama, language, and race in the U.S.* Oxford University Press.

Allen, J. R., Allen, S. F., Latrobe, K. H., Brand, M., Pfefferbaum, B., Elledge, B., Burton, T., & Guffey, M. (2012). The power of story. *Children and Libraries: The Journal of the Association for Library Service to Children, 10*(1), 44–49.

Allington, R. (2014). How reading volume affects both reading fluency and reading achievement. *International Electronic Journal of Elementary Education, 7*(1), 13–26.

Allington, R., & Cunningham, P. (2007). *Classrooms that work: They can all read and write.* Pearson.

Alvarez, J. (2006). *Finding miracles.* Laurel Leaf.

Anderson, L. A. (1999). *Speak.* Farrar, Straus, and Giroux.

Anderson, M., & Jiang, J. (2018). *Teens, social media and technology.* Pew Research Center. https://www.pewresearch.org/internet/2018/05/31/teens-social-media-technology-2018/

Anzaldua, G. E. (2002). Now let us shift . . . the path of conocimiento . . . inner work, public acts. In G. E. Anzaldua & A. Keating (Eds.), *This bridge we call home: Radical visions for transformation* (pp. 540–578). Routledge.

Asgedom, M. (2002). *Of beetles and angels: A boy's remarkable journey from a refugee camp to Harvard.* Little, Brown Books for Young Readers.

Atta, D. (2020). *Black flamingo.* Balzer + Bray.

Auerbach, S. (2012). Conceptualizing leadership for authentic partnerships: A continuum to inspire practice. In S. Auerbach (Ed.), *School leadership for authentic family and community partnerships* (pp. 29–52). Routledge.

Bagwell, C. L., & Schmidt, M. E. (2011). *Friendships in childhood and adolescence.* Guilford Press.

Baker-Bell, A. (2020). *Linguistic justice: Black language, literacy, identity and pedagogy.* Routledge.

Baker-Bell, A., Jones Stanbrough, R., & Everett, S. (2017). The stories they tell: Mainstream media, pedagogies of healing, and critical media literacy. *English Education, 49*(2), 130–152.

Beah, I. (2008). *A long way gone.* Sarah Crichton Books.

Beam, C. (2012). *I am J.* Little, Brown Books for Young Readers.

Bell, C. (2014). *El deafo.* Harry N. Abrams.

Bell, M. K. (2016). Teaching at the intersections. *Teaching Tolerance, 53*, 38–41.

Bertrand, D. G. (1999). *Trino's choice.* Arte Publico.

Betzalel, N., & Shechtman, Z. (2010). Bibliotherapy treatment for children with adjustment difficulties: A comparison of affective and cognitive bibliotherapy. *Journal of Creativity in Mental Health, 5*(4), 426–439.

Bishop, R. S. (1990). Mirrors, windows, and sliding glass doors. *Perspectives: Choosing and Using Books for the Classroom, 6*(3), 9–12.

Blum, H. T., Lipsett, L. R., & Yocum, D. J. (2002). Literature circles: A tool for self-determination in one middle school inclusive classroom. *Remedial and Special Education, 23*(2), 99–108.

Blume, J. (2010). *Tiger eyes.* Delacorte.

Boardman, A. G., Roberts, G., Vaughn, S., Wexler, J., Murray, C. S., & Kosanovich, M. (2008). *Effective instruction for adolescent struggling readers: A practice brief.* RMC Research Corporation.

Booth, D., & Rowsell, J. (2006). *The literacy principal: Leading, supporting, and assessing reading and writing initiatives* (2nd ed.). Stenhouse.

Borsheim-Black, C., Macaluso, M., & Petrone, R. (2014). Critical literature pedagogy: Teaching canonical literature for critical literacy. *Journal of Adolescent and Adult Literacy, 58*(2), 123–133.

Boston, G. H., & Baxley, T. (2007). Living the literature: Race, gender construction, and Black female adolescents. *Urban Education, 42*(5), 560–581.

Boulley, A. (2021). *Firekeeper's daughter.* Henry Holt.

Bowers-Campbell, J. (2011). Take it out of class: Exploring virtual literature circles. *Journal of Adolescent and Adult Literacy, 54*(8), 557–567.

Branje, S. J. T., van Aken, M. A. G., & van Lieshout, C. F. M. (2002). Relational support in families with adolescents. *Journal of Family Psychology, 16*(3), 351–362.

Brashares, A. (2003). *The sisterhood of the traveling pants.* Ember.

Brooks, W., & Browne, S. (2012). Towards a culturally situated reader response theory. *Children's Literature in Education, 43*, 74–85.

Brooks, W., Browne, S., & Hampton, G. (2008). "There ain't no accounting for what folks see in their own mirrors": Considering colorism within a Sharon Flake narrative. *Journal of Adolescent and Adult Literacy, 51*(8), 660–669.

Broughton, M. A. (2002). The performance and construction of subjectivities of early adolescent girls in book club discussion groups. *Journal of Literacy Research, 34*(1), 1–38.

Buckhanon, K. (2006). *Upstate.* St. Martin's Griffin.

Bureau of Labor Statistics. (2019). *American time use survey.* United States Department of Labor. https://www.bls.gov/charts/american-time-use/activity-leisure.htm

Callender, K. (2020). *Felix ever after.* Balzer + Bray.

Capper, C. A., & Young, M. D. (2015). The equity audit as the core of leading increasingly diverse schools and districts. In G. Theoharis & M. Scanlan (Eds.), *Leadership for increasingly diverse schools* (pp. 186–197). Routledge.

Caraballo, L., & Lyiscott, J. (2020). Collaborative inquiry: Youth, social action, and critical qualitative research. *Action Research, 18*(2), 194–211.

Carnine, D. W., Silbert, J., Kame'enui, E. J., & Tarver, S. G. (2010). *Direct instruction reading* (5th ed.). Pearson/Merrill.

Center on the Developing Child at Harvard University. (2016). *From best practices to breakthrough impacts: A science-based approach to building a more promising future for young children and families.* Author.

Cherry-Paul, S., & Johansen, D. (2019). *Breathing new life into book clubs: A practical guide for teachers.* Heinemann.

Choi, J., & Sachs, G. T. (2016). Adolescent multilinguals' engagement with religion in a book club. *Journal of Adolescent and Adult Literacy, 60*(4), 415–423.

Cobham, V. E. (2012). Do anxiety-disordered children need to come into the clinic for efficacious treatment? *Journal of Consulting and Clinical Psychology, 80*(3), 465–476.

Coleman, D., & Pimentel, S. (2012). *Revised publishers' criteria for the Common Core State Standards in English Language Arts and Literacy, Grades 3–12.* http://www.corestandards.org/assets/Publishers_Criteria_for_3-12.pdf

Collaborative for Academic, Social, and Emotional Learning (CASEL). (2020). *CASEL's SEL framework: What are the core competence areas and where are they promoted?* https://casel.org/wp-content/uploads/2020/12/CASEL-SEL-Framework-11.2020.pdf

Colwell, J., Woodward, L., & Hutchison, A. (2018). Out-of-school reading and literature discussion: An exploration of adolescents' participation in digital book clubs. *Online Learning, 22*(2), 221–247.

Comer, J. (2005). *Leave no child behind: Preparing today's youth for tomorrow's world.* Yale University Press.

Corr, C. A. (2004). Bereavement, grief, and mourning in death-related literature for children. *OMEGA, 48*, 337–363.

Côté-Lussier, C., & Fitzpatrick, C. (2016). Feelings of safety at school, socioemotional functioning, and classroom engagement. *Journal of Adolescent Health, 58*(5), 543–550.

Craft, J. (2019). *New kid.* Quill Tree.

Cronin, A. (2016). Student-led conferences: Resources for educators. *Edutopia.* https://www.edutopia.org/blog/student-led-conferences-resources-ashley-cronin

Crothers, S. M. (1916). A literary clinic. *Atlantic Monthly.* https://www.theatlantic.com/magazine/archive/1916/09/literary-clinic/609754/

Curtis, C. P. (2006). *Bucking the sarge.* Laurel Leaf.

Daniels, H. (2002). *Literature circles* (2nd ed.). Stenhouse.

Davidson, D. (2005). *Jason and Kyra.* Little, Brown Books for Young Readers.

DeVries, D., Brennan, Z., Lankin, M., Morse, R., Rix, B., & Beck, T. (2017). Healing with books: A literature review of bibliotherapy used with children and youth who have experienced trauma. *Therapeutic Recreation Journal, 51*(1), 48–74.

DiAngelo, R. (2018). *White fragility: Why it's so hard for white people to talk about racism.* Beacon Press.

Diaz, J. (2008). *The brief wondrous life of Oscar Wao*. Riverhead.

Dobson, A. (2012). Listening: The new democratic deficit. *Political Studies, 60*(4), 843–859.

Draper, S. (1996). *Tears of a tiger*. Atheneum Books for Young Readers.

Draper, S. (2001). *Romiette and Julio*. Simon Pulse.

Duimstra, L. (2003). Teaching and name-calling: Using books to help students cope. *Teacher Librarian, 31*(2), 8–11.

Duncan-Andrade, J. M. (2009). Note to educators: Hope required when growing roses in concrete. *Harvard Educational Review, 79*(2), 181–194.

Duyvis, C. (2016). *On the edge of gone*. Abrams.

Early, M., & Marshall, S. (2008). Adolescent ESL students' interpretation and appreciation of literary text: A case study of multimodality. *Canadian Modern Language Review, 64*(3), 377–397.

Education Trust. (2020). *Social, emotional, and academic development through an equity lens*. https://edtrust.org/wp-content/uploads/2014/09/Social-Emotional-and-Academic-Development-Through-an-Equity-Lens-August-6-2020.pdf

Elhess, M., & Egbert, J. (2015). Literature circles as support for language development. *English Teaching Forum, 53*(3), 13–21.

Elmore, G. M., & Huebner, E. S. (2010). Adolescents' satisfaction with school experiences: Relationships with demographics, attachment relationships, and school engagement behavior. *Psychology in the Schools, 47*(6), 525–537.

Eppley, K. (2019). Close reading: What is reading for? *Curriculum Inquiry, 49*(3), 338–355.

Espinoza, M. (2009). A case study of the production of educational sanctuary in one migrant classroom. *Pedagogies: An International Journal, 4*, 44–62.

Evans, K. S. (1996). Creating spaces for equity? The role of positioning in peer-led literature discussions. *Language Arts, 73*(3), 194–202.

Fisher, M. T. (2006). Earning "dual degrees": Black bookstores as alternative knowledge spaces. *Anthropology and Education Quarterly, 37*(1), 83–99.

Fleischman, P. (2004). *Seedfolks*. HarperTrophy.

Ford, D. Y., Walters, N. M., & Byrd, J. A. (2019). I want to read about me: Engaging and empowering gifted Black girls using multicultural literature and bibliotherapy. *Gifted Child Today, 42*(1), 53–57.

Forgan, J. W. (2002). Using bibliotherapy to teach problem solving. *Intervention in School and Clinic, 38*, 75–82.

Foster, J. M. (2015). Addressing fear in child victims of sexual abuse. *Counseling Today*. https://ct.counseling.org/2015/01/addressing-fear-in-child-victims-of-sexual-abuse

Frank, D. I., & Cannon, E. P. (2009). Creative approaches to serving LGBTQ youth in schools. *Journal of School Counseling, 7*(35), 1–25.

Frankel, K. K., & Brooks, M. D. (2018). Why the "struggling reader" label is harmful (and what educators can do about it). *Journal of Adolescent and Adult Literacy, 62*(1), 111–114.

Freire, P. (1993). *Pedagogy of the oppressed*. Continuum.

Freire, P., & Macedo, D. (1987). *Literacy: Reading the word and the world*. Bergin & Garvey.

Furman, W., Low, S., & Ho, M. J. (2009). Romantic experience and psychosocial adjustment in middle adolescence. *Journal of Clinical Child and Adolescent Psychology, 38*(1), 75–90.

Gabriel, M. L., Roxas, K. C., & Becker, K. (2017). Meeting, knowing, and affirming Spanish-speaking immigrant families through successful culturally responsive family engagement. *Journal of Family Diversity in Education, 2*(3), 1–18.

Gibbons, L. C., Dail, J. S., & Stallworth, B. J. (2006). Young adult literature in the English curriculum today: Classroom teachers speak out. *ALAN Review, 33*(3), 53–61.

Gino, A. (2017). *George.* Scholastic.

Ginsberg, B. (2012). *Episodes: Scenes from life, love, and autism.* Square Fish.

Ginwright, S. (2016). *Hope and healing in urban education: How urban activists and teachers are reclaiming matters of the heart.* Routledge.

Ginwright, S. (2018). *The future of healing: Shifting from trauma informed care to healing centered engagement.* https://ginwright.medium.com/the-future-of-healing-shifting-from-trauma-informed-care-to-healing-centered-engagement-634f557ce69c

Ginwright, S., & James, T. (2002). From assets to agents of change: Social justice, organizing, and youth development. *New Directions for Youth Development, 96*, 27–46.

Glasgow, K. (2019). *How to make friends with the dark.* Delacorte.

Glenn, W. J., & Ginsberg, R. (2016). Resisting readers' identity (re)construction across English and young adult literature course contexts. *Research in the Teaching of English, 51*(1), 84–105.

Goodwin, B., & Jones, L. M. (2020). A "write" way to address trauma. *Educational Leadership, 78*(2), 74–75.

Gorski, P. (2013). *Reaching and teaching students in poverty: Strategies for erasing the opportunity gap.* Teachers College Press.

Gorski, P. (2020). How trauma-informed are we, really? *Educational Leadership, 78*(2), 14–19.

Graham, S., & Hebert, M. A. (2010). *Writing to read: Evidence for how writing can improve reading. A Carnegie Corporation Time to Act Report.* Alliance for Excellent Education.

Graham, S., Munniksma, A., & Juvonen, J. (2013). Psychosocial benefits of cross-ethnic friendships in urban middle schools. *Child Development, 85*(2), 469–483.

Graham, S., & Perin, D. (2007). *Writing next: Effective strategies to improve writing of adolescents in middle and high schools.* Alliance for Excellent Education.

Green, T. L. (2017). Community-based equity audits: A practical approach for educational leaders to support equitable community-school improvements. *Educational Administration Quarterly, 53*(1), 3–39.

Greene, D. T. (2016). "We need more 'US' in schools!!": Centering Black adolescent girls' literacy and language practices in online school spaces. *The Journal of Negro Education, 85*(3), 274–289.

Guerra, P. L., & Nelson, S. W. (2013). Latino parent involvement: Seeing what has always been there. *Journal of School Leadership, 23*(3), 424–455.

Guthrie, J. T., Wigfield, A., & You, W. (2012). Instructional contexts for engagement and achievement in reading. In S. L. Christenson, A. L. Reschly, & C. Wylie (Eds.), *Handbook of research on student engagement* (pp. 601–634). Springer.

Ha, R. (2020). *Almost American girl: An illustrated memoir.* Balzer + Bray.

Hall, L. A., Johnson, A. S., Juzwik, M. M., Wortham, S. E. F., & Mosley, M. (2010). Teacher identity in the context of literacy teaching: Three explorations of classroom positioning and interaction in secondary schools. *Teaching and Teacher Education, 26*(2), 234–243.

Handsfield, L. J., & Valente, P. (2021). Pedagogies of closeness: Humanizing small-group comprehension instruction. *Language Arts, 98*(4), 201–207.

Harvey, S., & Ward, A. (2017). *From striving to thriving: How to grow confident, capable readers.* Scholastic.

Hill, M. L. (2009). Wounded healing: Forming a storytelling community in hip-hop lit. *Teachers College Record, 111*(1), 248–293.

Hoffman, J. V. (2017). What if "just right" is just wrong? The unintended consequences of leveling readers. *The Reading Teacher (71)*3, 265–273.

Holman, F. (1986). *Slake's limbo.* Aladdin.

hooks, b. (1991). Theory as liberatory practice. *Yale Journal of Law and Feminism, 4*(1), 1–12.

hooks, b. (1994). *Teaching to transgress: Education as the practice of freedom.* Routledge.

Hoose, P. (2010). *Claudette Colvin: Twice toward justice.* Square Fish.

Hucks, D. C. (2014). *New visions of collective achievement: The cross-generational schooling experiences of African American males.* Sense Publishers.

Ireland, J. (2018). *Dread nation.* Balzer + Bray.

Ivey, G., & Johnston, P. (2013). Engagement with young adult literature: Outcomes and processes. *Reading Research Quarterly, 48*(3), 255–275.

Ivey, G., & Johnston, P. (2017). Emerging adolescence in engaged reading communities. *Language Arts, 94*(3), 159–169.

Ivey, G., & Johnston, P. (2018). Engaging disturbing books. *Journal of Adolescent and Adult Literacy, 62*(2), 143–150.

Janks, H. (2010). *Literacy and power.* Routledge.

Jewell, T. (2020). *This book is anti-racist: 20 lessons on how to wake up, take action, and do the work.* Francis Lincoln Children's Books.

Johnson, L. P. (2017). Writing the self: Black queer youth challenge heteronormative ways of being in an after-school writing club. *Research in the Teaching of English, 52*(1), 13–33.

Johnson, L. P., & Eubanks, E. (2015). Anthem or nah? Culturally relevant writing instruction and community. *Voices from the Middle, 23*(2), 31–36.

Jones, S. (2020). Ending curriculum violence. *Learning for Justice, 64,* 47–50.

Kaler-Jones, C. (2020, May 7). *When SEL is used as another form of policing.* Medium. https://medium.com/@justschools/when-sel-is-used-as-another-form-of-policing-fa53cf85dce4

Kay, M. R. (2018). *Not light but fire: How to lead meaningful race conversations in the classroom.* Stenhouse.

Kenny, R., Dooley, B. A., & Fitzgerald, A. (2014). Interpersonal relationships and emotional distress in adolescence. *Journal of Adolescence, 36*(2), 351–360.

Ketch, A. (2005). Conversation: The comprehension connection. *The Reading Teacher, 59*(1), 8–13.

Khan, S. (2019). *The love and lies of Rukhsana Ali.* Scholastic Press.

Khan-Cullors, P., & bandele, a. (2020). *When they call you a terrorist: A story of Black Lives Matter and the power to change the world* (young adult ed.). Wednesday Books.

Khorram, A. (2018). *Darius the great is not okay.* Penguin.

King, A. S. (2013). *Reality boy*. Little, Brown Books for Young Readers.

Kinney, J. (2007). *Diary of a wimpy kid*. Amulet.

Kirkland, D. E. (2010). English(es) in urban contexts: Politics, pluralism, and possibilities. *English Education, 42*(3), 293–306.

Knifsend, C. A., & Juvonen, J. (2013). Social identity complexity, crossethnic friendships, and intergroup attitudes in urban middle schools. *Child Development, 85*(2), 709–712.

Krashen, S. D. (2011). *Free voluntary reading*. Libraries Unlimited.

Kunzel, B., & Hardesty, C. (2006). *The teen-centered book club: Readers into leaders*. Libraries Unlimited.

Kuperminc, G. P., Darnell, A. J., & Alvarez-Jimenez, A. (2008). Parent involvement in the academic adjustment of Latino middle and high school youth: Teacher expectations and school belonging as mediators. *Journal of Adolescence, 31*(4), 469–483.

Ladson-Billings, G. (2007). Pushing past the achievement gap: An essay on the language of deficit. *Journal of Negro Education, 76*(3), 316–323.

Ladson-Billings, G. (2014). Culturally relevant pedagogy 2.0: A.k.a the remix. *Harvard Educational Review, 84*(1), 74–84.

Lee, C. D., & Spratley, A. (2010). *Reading in the disciplines: The challenges of adolescent literacy*. Carnegie Corporation of New York.

Lee, L. (2020). *I'll be the one*. Katherine Tegen Boks.

Lehman, C., & Roberts, K. (2013). *Falling in love with close reading: Lessons for analyzing texts—and life*. Heinemann.

Lenski, S. D., Wham, M. A., Johns, J. L., & Caskey, M. M. (2007). *Reading and learning strategies: Middle grades through high school* (3rd ed.). Kendall/Hunt.

Leonardo, Z. (2004). Critical social theory and transformative knowledge: The functions of criticism in quality education. *Educational Researcher, 33*(6), 11–18.

Lesko, N. (2012). *Act your age! A cultural construction of adolescence* (2nd ed.). Routledge.

Lewis, M. A., & Petrone, R. (2010). "Although adolescence need not be violent . . .": Preservice teachers' connections between "adolescence" and literacy curriculum. *Journal of Adolescent and Adult Literacy, 53*(5), 398–407.

Lewis, M. A., & Zisselsberger, M. A. (2018). Scaffolding and inequitable participation in linguistically diverse book clubs. *Reading Research Quarterly, 54*(2), 167–186.

Lindsey, M., Sheftall, A. H., Xiao, Y., & Joe, S. (2019). Trends of suicidal behaviors among high school students in the United States, 1991–2017. *Pediatrics, 144*(5), 1–10.

Llopart, M., & Esteban-Guitart, M. (2018). Funds of knowledge in 21st century societies: Inclusive educational practices for under-represented students. A literature review. *Journal of Curriculum Studies, 50*(2), 145–161.

Lo, M. (2012). *Huntress*. Little, Brown Books for Young Readers.

Lorde, A. (1982). *Zami: A new spelling of my name*. Crossing Press.

Lorde, A. (2007). *Sister outsider: Essays and speeches*. Crossing Press.

Love, B. (2019). *We want to do more than survive: Abolitionist teaching and the pursuit of educational freedom*. Beacon Press.

Luke, A. (2000). Critical literacy in Australia: A matter of context and standpoint. *Journal of Adolescent and Adult Literacy, 43*(5), 448–461.

Luke, A. (2012). Critical literacy: Foundational notes. *Theory into Practice, 51*(1), 4–11.

Luke, A., & Woods, A. (2009). Critical literacies in schools: A primer. *Voices from the Middle, 17*(2), 9–18.

MacDonald, J., Vallance, D., & McGrath, M. (2012). An evaluation of a collaborative bibliotherapy scheme delivered via a library service. *Journal of Psychiatric and Mental Health Nursing, 20*(10), 857–865.

Magoon, K. (2013). *Fire in the streets.* Aladdin.

Malmgren, K. W., & Trezek, B. J. (2009). Literacy instruction for secondary students with disabilities. *Focus on Exceptional Children, 41*(6), 1–12.

Manzano, S. (2014). *The revolution of Evelyn Serrano.* Scholastic.

Marchand-Martella, N. E., & Martella, R. C. (2013). Explicit instruction. In W. L. Heward (Ed.), *Exceptional children* (10th ed., pp. 166–168). Pearson/Merrill.

Marchand-Martella, N. E., Martella, R. C., Modderman, S. L., Petersen, H. M., & Pan, S. (2013). Key areas of effective adolescent literacy programs. *Education and Treatment of Children, 36*(1), 161–184.

Marzano, R. (2010). The science of teaching/Teaching inference. *Educational Leadership, 67*(7), 80–81.

Matias, C. E. (2016). *Feeling white: Whiteness, emotionality, and education.* Sense Publishers.

Matias, C. E., & Mackey, J. (2016). Breakin' down whiteness in antiracist teaching: Introducing critical whiteness pedagogy. *Urban Review, 48*, 32–50.

McGee, E. O., & Stovall, D. (2015). Reimagining critical race theory in education: Mental health, healing, and the pathway to liberatory praxis. *Educational Theory, 65*(5), 491–511.

McKenna, M. C., Conradi, K., Lawrence, C., Jang, B. G., & Meyer, J. P. (2012). Reading attitudes of middle school students: Results of a U.S. survey. *Reading Research Quarterly, 47*(3), 283–306.

Metz, M. (2020). Amplifying academic talk: High quality discussions in the language of comfort. *The English Journal, 109*(4), 55–61.

Minahan, J. (2019). Trauma-informed teaching strategies. *Educational Leadership, 77*(2), 30–35.

Moje, E. B., & Luke, A. (2009). Literacy and identity: Examining the metaphors in history and contemporary research. *Reading Research Quarterly, 44*(4), 415–437.

Moll, L. C. (1992). Bilingual classroom studies and community analysis: Some recent trends. *Educational Researcher, 21*(2), 20–24.

Morrell, E. (2008). *Critical literacy and urban youth: Pedagogies of access, dissent, and liberation.* Routledge.

Morrison, T. (2007). *The bluest eye.* Vintage.

Muhammad, G. E., & Haddix, M. (2016). Centering Black girls' literacies: A review of literature on the multiple ways of knowing of Black girls. *English Education, 48*(4), 299–336.

Myers, W. D. (1996). *Slam!* Scholastic.

National Endowment for the Arts. (2007). *To read or not to read: A question of national consequence.* Research Report 47. Author.

National Institute for Literacy. (2007). *What content-area teachers should know about adolescent literacy.* National Institute of Child Health and Human Development.

Nazario, S. (2007). *Enrique's journey.* Random House.

Nieto, S. (2010). *Language, culture, and teaching: Critical perspectives* (2nd ed.). Routledge.

Nieto, S. (2016). *Finding joy in teaching students of diverse backgrounds: Culturally responsive and socially just practices in U.S. classrooms.* Heinemann.

Nouri, A., & Sajjadi, S. M. (2014). Emancipatory pedagogy in practice: Aims, principles and curriculum orientation. *International Journal of Critical Pedagogy, 5*(2), 76–85.

OECD. (2011). *PISA 2009 results: Students on line: Vol. 6. Digital technologies and performance.* Author. https://www.oecd.org/pisa/pisaproducts/48270093.pdf

Older, D. J. (2016). *Shadowshaper.* Scholastic.

Pan, E. X. R. (2019). *The astonishing color of after.* Little, Brown Books for Young Readers.

Panjwani, N. (2011). Saving our future: James Comer and the School Development Program. *Yale Journal of Biology and Medicine, 84*(2), 139–143.

Paris, D. (2009). "They're in my culture, they speak the same way": African American language in multiethnic high schools. *Harvard Educational Review, 79*(3), 428–448.

Paris, D. (2012). Culturally sustaining pedagogy: A needed change in stance, terminology, and practice. *Educational Researcher, 41*(3), 93–97.

Paris, D., & Alim, S. (2014). What are we seeking to sustain through culturally sustaining pedagogy? A loving critique forward. *Harvard Educational Review, 84*(1), 85–100.

Park, S., & Schepp, K. G. (2015). A systematic review of research on children of alcoholics: Their inherent resilience and vulnerability. *Journal of Child and Family Studies, 24*(5), 1222–1231.

Paulsen, G. (2006). *Hatchet.* Simon & Schuster.

Pehrsson, D., Allen, V. B., Folger, W. A., McMillen, P. S., & Lowe, I. (2007). Bibliotherapy with preadolescents experiencing divorce. *Family Journal: Counseling and Therapy for Couples and Families, 15*(4), 409–414.

Pennebaker, J. W., & Smyth, J. M. (2016). *Opening up by writing it down: How expressive writing improves health and eases emotional pain* (3rd ed.). Guilford.

Peralta, C. (2019). Why are we still blaming families in 2019? *The Reading Teacher, 72*(5), 670–674.

Pike, C. (1994). *The last vampire.* Simon & Schuster.

Pitman, G. E. (2019). *The Stonewall riots: Coming out in the streets.* Abrams.

Pittman, P., & Honchell, B. (2014). Literature discussion: Encouraging reading interest and comprehension in struggling middle school readers. *Journal of Language and Literacy Education, 10*(2), 118–133.

Polleck, J. (2011a). Adolescent literature book clubs: A forum for cultivation of peer relationships with urban adolescent females. *ALAN Review, 38*(1), 76–95.

Polleck, J. (2011b). Constructing dressing rooms in urban schools: Understanding family through book clubs with Latino and African American female adolescents. *Journal of Poetry Therapy, 24*(3), 139–155.

Polleck, J. (2016). Bring texts to life: Using afterschool book clubs as a way to address and reinforce the Common Core standards for literacy with urban adolescents. In J. Hayn, J. Kaplan, & A. Nolen (Eds.), *Implementing Common Core literacy standards through young adult literature* (pp. 97–113). Roman & Littlefield.

Polleck, J., & Epstein, T. (2015). Affirmation, analysis, and agency: Book clubs as spaces for critical conversations with young adolescent women of color. *Reading Horizons, 54*(1), 78–107.

Polleck, J., & Smith, A. (2021). Bridging islands to build a continent: Harnessing the power of digital book clubs during the COVID-19 pandemic. In K. J. Fasching-Varner, S. T. Bickmore, D. G. Hays, P. G. Schrader, D. L. Carlson, & D. Anagostopoulous (Eds.), *The corona chronicles: On leadership, processes, commitments, and hope in uncertain times* (pp. 77–84). DIO Press.

Poulin, F., & Chan, A. (2010). Friendship stability and change in childhood and adolescence. *Developmental Review, 30,* 257–272.

Probst, R. E. (2004). *Response and analysis* (2nd ed.). Heinemann.

Quinn, D. M., & Polikoff, M. (2017). *Summer learning loss: What is it, and what can we do about it?* Brookings. https://www.brookings.edu/research/summer-learning-loss-what-is-it-and-what-can-we-do-about-it/

Rawson, K. A., Dunlosky, J., & Thiede, K. W. (2000). The rereading effect: Meta-comprehension accuracy improves across reading trials. *Memory and Cognition, 28*(6), 1004–1010.

Reutzel, D. R., Petscher, Y., & Spichtig, A. (2012). Exploring the valued added of a guided, silent reading intervention: Effects on struggling third-grade readers' achievement. *Journal of Education Research, 105,* 404–415.

Reynolds, J., & Kiely, B. (2015). *All American boys.* Atheneum.

Riesco, H. S. (2021). Positioning YA lit as mentor texts for social and emotional literacy. *Voices from the Middle, 28*(4), 60–64.

Riley, K. (2015). Enacting critical literacy in English classrooms: How a teacher learning community supported critical inquiry. *Journal of Adolescent and Adult Literacy, 58*(5), 417–425.

Riley, K., & Cohen, S. (2018). In Philadelphia, teacher book groups are the engines of change. *Rethinking Schools, 32*(3), 38–45.

Rodriguez, G. M. (2013). Power and agency in education: Exploring the pedagogical dimensions of funds of knowledge. *Review of Research in Education, 37,* 87–120.

Rosenblatt, L. M. (1994). *The reader, the text, and the poem: The transactional theory of the literary world.* Southern Illinois University Press.

Roskos, K., & Neuman, S. B. (2014). Best practices in reading: A 21st century update. *Reading Teacher, 67*(7), 507–511.

Roy, A. (2008). *The god of small things.* Random House.

Rubio Cancino, E. M., & Buitrago Cruz, C. P. (2019). Exploring the use of bibliotherapy with English as a second language students. *English Language Teaching, 12*(7), 98–106.

Saeed, A. (2016). *Written in the stars.* Speak.

Saldana, R., Jr. (2020). (Mis)understanding culture: Literacy through lived experience. *English Journal, 109*(3), 50–53.

Sanacore, J. (2013). "Slow down, you move too fast": Literature circles as reflective practice. *Clearing House, 86,* 116–120.

Santiago, E. (2006). *When I was a Puerto Rican: A memoir.* Da Capo Press.

Santori, D., & Belfatti, M. (2017). Do text-dependent questions need to be teacher dependent? Close reading from another angle. *Reading Teacher, 70*(6), 649–657.

Saperstein, J. A. (2010). *Atypical: Life with Asperger's in 20⅓ chapters.* Perigee.

Sapphire. (1997). *Push: A novel*. Vintage.

Sarigianides, S. T. (2012). Tensions in teaching adolescence/ts: Analyzing resistances in a young adult literature course. *Journal of Adolescent and Adult Literacy, 56*(3), 222–230.

Schieble, M., Vetter, A., & Martin, K. M. (2020). *Classroom talk for social change: Critical conversations in English language arts*. Teachers College Press.

Schreuder, M. C., & Savitz, R. S. (2020). Exploring adolescent motivation to read with an online YA book club. *Literacy Research and Instruction, 59*(3), 260–275.

Sharp, P. (2001). *Nurturing emotional literacy. A practical guide for teachers, parents and those in the caring profession*. Routledge.

Shlasko, G. D. (2005). Queer (v.) pedagogy. *Equity and Excellence in Education, 38*, 123–134.

Shusterman, N. (2017). *Scythe*. Simon & Schuster.

Simmons, D. (2019). Why we can't afford whitewashed social-emotional learning. *ASCD Education Update, 61*(4). https://www.ascd.org/el/articles/why-we-cant -afford-whitewashed-social-emotional-learning.

Simmons, D. (2020a). Confronting inequity/The trauma we don't see. *Educational Leadership, 77*(8), 88–89.

Simmons, D. (2020b). Confronting inequity/Healing Black students' pain. *Educational Leadership, 78*(2), 80–81.

Simmons, D. (2020c). *If we aren't addressing racism, we aren't addressing trauma* [Blog post]. https://inservice.ascd.org/if-we-arent-addressing-racism-we-arent-address ing-trauma/?fbclid=IwAR3fKyIJpO3IdXg0TzbGNGtGFwEZX5FtDjruNPR -lhiUwjKlwUExohhuVWI

Skrla, L. E., McKenzie, K. B., & Scheurich, J. J. (Eds.). (2009). *Using equity audits to create equitable and excellent schools*. Corwin.

Smith, A. (2020). *Empowerment and revelation through literature: A digital book club for post-incarceration* [Unpublished doctoral dissertation]. Columbia University, Teachers College.

Souljah, S. (2005). *The coldest winter ever*. Washington Square Press.

Stahl, S., & Nagy, W. (2006). *Teaching word meanings*. Erlbaum.

Staley, S., & Leonardi, B. (2016). Leaning in to discomfort: Preparing literacy teachers for gender and sexual diversity. *Research in the Teaching of English, 51*(2), 209–229.

Stewart-Mitchell, J. (2020). Blogging about books. *Educational Leadership, 77*(7), 68–73.

Stice, E., Rohde, P., Gau, J., & Ochner, C. (2011). Relation of depression to perceived social support: Results from a randomized adolescent depression prevention trial. *Behaviour Research and Therapy, 49*(5), 361–366.

Stork, F. X. (2011). *Marcelo in the real world*. Scholastic.

Strong, Z. H., & McMain, E. M. (2020). Social emotional learning for social emotional justice: A conceptual framework for education in the midst of the pandemics. *Northwest Journal of Teacher Education, 15*(2). https://pdxscholar.library .pdx.edu/cgi/viewcontent.cgi?article=1237&context=nwjte

Sulzer, M. A., & Thein, A. H. (2016). Reconsidering the hypothetical adolescent in evaluating and teaching young adult literature. *Journal of Adolescent and Adult Literacy, 60*(2), 163–171.

Sutcliffe, W. (2017). *We see everything*. Bloomsbury.

Taber, N., Woloshyn, V., & Lane, L. (2012). Food chains, frenemies, and revenge fantasies: Related fiction to life in a girls' book club. *Brock Education, 22*(1), 41–55.

Tanner, S. J. (2019). Whiteness is a white problem: Whiteness in English education. *English Education, 51*(2), 182–199.

Tatum, A. (2013). *Fearless voices: Engaging a new generation of African American adolescent male writers.* Scholastic.

Tervalon, M., & Murray-Garcia, J. (1998). Cultural humility versus cultural competence: A critical distinction in defining physician training outcomes in multicultural education. *Journal of Health Care for the Poor and Underserved, 9*(2), 117–125.

Thein, A. H., Guise, M., & Sloan, D. L. (2011). Problematizing literature circles as forums for discussion of multicultural and political texts. *Journal of Adolescent and Adult Literacy, 55*(1), 15–24.

Thierry, J. (2020). *A kid's book about systemic racism.* A Kid's Book About.

Thompson, J. (2018). *Text dependent analysis: The need for a shift in instruction and curriculum.* Center for Assessment.

Tijms, J., Stoop, M. A., & Polleck, J. N. (2018). Bibliotherapeutic book club intervention to promote reading skills and social–emotional competencies in low SES community-based high schools: A randomised controlled trial. *Journal of Research in Reading, 41*(3), 525–545.

Tukhareli, N. (2011). Bibliotherapy in a library setting: Reaching out to vulnerable youth. *Partnership: The Canadian Journal of Library and Information Practice and Research*, 6(1). https://doi.org/10.21083/partnership.v6i1.1402

Twenge, J. M., Martin, G. N., & Spitzberg, B. H. (2019). Trends in U.S. adolescents' media use, 1976–2016: The rise of digital media, the decline of TV, and the (near) demise of print. *Psychology of Popular Media, 8*(4), 329–345.

Twenge, J. M., Spitzberg, B. H., & Campbell, W. K. (2019). Less in-person social interaction with peers among U.S. adolescents in the 21st century and links to loneliness. *Journal of Social and Personal Relationships, 36*(6), 1892–1913.

Tynes, B. M., Willis, H. A., Stewart, A. M., & Hamilton, M. W. (2019). Race-related traumatic events online and mental health among adolescents of color. *Journal of Adolescent Health, 65*, 371–377.

UNESCO. (2017). *Inclusion in education.* https://en.unesco.org/themes/inclusion-in-education

Valencia, R. R. (2010). *Dismantling contemporary deficit thinking: Educational thought and practice.* Routledge.

Van Duinen, D. V., Hamilton, E. R., & Rumohr-Voskuil, G. (2017). Challenging constructions together: Implications of a mother-daughter book club for classroom practice. *Voices from the Middle, 24*(4), 67–73.

Veronneau, M. H., & Dishion, T. J. (2011). Middle school friendships and academic achievement in early adolescence: A longitudinal analysis. *Journal of Early Adolescence, 31*(1), 99–124.

Vyas, S. (2004). Exploring bicultural identities of Asian students through the analytic window of a literature club. *Journal of Adolescent and Adult Literacy, 48*(1), 12–23.

Wade, R., Jr., Shea, J. A., Rubin, D., & Wood, J. (2014). Adverse childhood experiences of low-income youth. *Pediatrics, 134*(1), 13–20.

Waitoller, F. R., & King Thorius, K. A. (2016). Cross-pollinating culturally sustaining pedagogy and universal design for learning: Towards an inclusive pedagogy that accounts for dis/ability. *Harvard Educational Review, 86*(3), 366–389.

Wender, E. (2017). Making a case for emotion in the Common Core understanding of close reading. *Journal of Curriculum Theorizing, 32*(1), 19–33.

Williams, S. M. (2009). *The impact of collaborative, scaffolded learning in K–12 schools: A meta-analysis.* Metiri Group.

Williams-Garcia, R. (1998). *Like sisters on the homefront.* Puffin Books.

Willingham, D. T. (2015). *Raising kids who read: What parents and teachers can do.* Jossey-Bass.

Willis, J. (2017). The neuroscience of joyful education. *Educational Leadership, 64.* https://www.psychologytoday.com/files/attachments/4141/the-neuroscience-joyful -education-judy-willis-md.pdf

Wilson, S., & Thornton, S. (2007/2008). "The factor that makes us more effective teachers": Two pre-service primary teachers' experience of bibliotherapy. *Mathematics Teacher Education and Development, 9,* 21–35.

Winn, M. T., & Johnson, L. P. (2011). *Writing instruction in the culturally relevant classroom.* National Council of Teachers of English.

Wiseman, A. M. (2011). Family involvement for adolescents in a community poetry workshop: Influences of parent roles and life context variables. *School Community Journal, 21*(2), 99–118.

Wizner, J. (2008). *Spanking Shakespeare.* Ember.

Index

About the Author

Dr. Jody Polleck is an associate professor and program coordinator for literacy at Hunter College–City University of New York (CUNY). She began her work with adolescents in 1994 as an outreach counselor for displaced youth in Washington, DC. In 1999, she received her master's in English education and worked as a high school reading and English teacher for emerging readers and writers. In 2002, Jody received National Board Certification for adolescent English language arts, and in 2003, she accepted a full fellowship to New York University, where she completed her doctoral degree in English education. Jody continues to teach high school students through the CUNY College Now Program and was a 2019 Fulbright scholar in the Netherlands. Her research focuses on differentiated and culturally responsive–sustaining literacy instruction. She has published in over 25 books and journals, including *ALAN Review*, *Contemporary Issues in Technology and Teacher Education*, *English Journal*, *High School Journal*, *Journal of Teaching Writing*, *Literacy Research and Instruction*, *Preventing School Failure*, *Reading and Writing Quarterly*, *Reading Horizons*, and *Teacher Education Quarterly*.